TRANSLATION BY
FAITH

Dr. Bruce D. Allen
and
Michael Van Vlymen

ISBN 13: 13: 978-0996701419
ISBN 10: 0996701419

INTRODUCTION

The On the 13th of September, 2015 I had a visitation by the Lord Jesus. In this encounter I found myself standing before Jesus as He was standing on a hilltop overlooking the Temple in the New Jerusalem in heaven. He was revealing Himself as the King of Glory with a multifaceted/jeweled crown upon His head and a red robe. Immediately upon seeing him I fell down as a dead man at His feet. I had no strength left in me. As I prostrated myself at His feet I could do nothing but worship him for who He is and for all that He has so graciously given me over the years; all the successes and failures, all the joys and sorrows, all the revelation and experiences/encounters; I could do nothing but with joy and reverence place everything at His feet. I knew in that moment that all that I am - all that I have is His.

This continued for some time before I heard the Lord's voice say to me 'Arise and look'. He then extended His hand to me and I immediately received strength and was able to stand.

I was then shown vast multitudes - millions before the temple of God in heaven. From the vantage point of this hill overlooking the Temple I was able to witness a very unusual sight. I turned to both the left and right as far as the eye could see there were millions of people gathering, and yet the silence I witnessed was in and of itself awe inspiring! I knew there was about to be a proclamation of great importance that was going to affect the course of history!

As I was pondering what this pronouncement might be I witnessed an innumerable company of chariots of fire coming from above the temple out of the midst of what looked like clouds. I instinctively realized they had been released from the presence of the Father.

As this was taking place I saw a man approaching. He was walking up a golden path to the hilltop where we were standing. In his arms I noticed he was carrying a large book held tightly against his chest.

Immediately I knew by the spirit this was Enoch. As Enoch approached I was at once overjoyed and curious as I've longed to more fully understand and gaze into the mysteries he has witnessed in his walk with the Lord. I had hundreds of questions I wanted to ask.

As he came near I was surprised that he was not a very tall man. I had envisioned him as someone that would be quite large and muscular. I greeted him and was surprised when he greeted me by name! I had been told before that all in heaven know and recognize those who belong to the Lord. When we get there, we will recognize everyone we meet even though we have never met before.

Enoch then handed me the book he was holding. He said it was the book of mysteries the Lord had given him while he walked with the Lord for 300 years on this earth. As I grasped the book I was aware that it was a living thing! It emitted a power that was tangible and quite frankly, rather frightening! I was in awe of this 'living manuscript' that I was holding and yet my spirit instantly bore witness that this was right.

Enoch then said something that stunned me! He said, "Take the book and finish it. What I began while I was on the earth must now be completed in this generation."
I didn't know what to say! I was shaking and I responded with the first thing that came to mind: I asked him to lay his hand upon me and bless me.

He immediately responded and said, "No! There is no need of an impartation or blessing from me as the Lord Jesus Himself has already blessed you and commissioned you. I will however be in prayer for you."

As he spoke this I turned to the Lord and Jesus spoke with great compassion and authority, "Go and do all I've commanded you. I have given you insight and you have received my purposes and desire for your life. Now I give you understanding. As you have met Enoch this night and received his book of mysteries so too you shall receive of his mantel that has been prepared for this day. Move forward in faith and do not hold back, now the hour has come for My Glory to be revealed in you. Trust me to perform all that I said I would do for it shall surely come to pass now."

I share this to encourage you. This visitation was not about me! This is a promise to all in this generation that will surrender themselves to the purposes of God and the Book of Destiny for their life. This is for you!

Since this visitation our ministry focus has heightened and increased to share and impart the revelation we have received from the Lord regarding Translation by Faith (See Hebrews 11:5). We have been encouraged to witness in the past 5 schools that the Lord in His grace and mercy has been releasing His people in a way never before seen. There truly is a grace in this season for you to receive and be activated to walk in the realm of the supernatural as never before.

I want to encourage you – passionately pursue the Lord and seek His face. We are in a season of acceleration and release as never before. This is your hour, your day of encounter and visitation. You have struggled and plodded on through thick and thin, now you are about to come into His rest and victory!

Bruce Allen

A PRAYER

Father, As we seek to know you and your will in our lives, as we desire to lay hold of all those things that Jesus paid such a high price to give to us, let your Holy Spirit lead us and guide us into all truth. Father cover us in the blood of Jesus and set a hedge about us to keep us safe in the center of your will. Let your angels have charge over us and according Colossians 1:9, let Wisdom, Revelation and Knowledge of your will be established in us . Father teach us about this thing called translation by faith. We yield to you and your will. Teach us and give us lessons and experiences every day. Make the supernatural things of your Kingdom normal to us. Teach us to move supernaturally through time and space for the cause of the Gospel, and help us to lay down all the weights that would so easily beset us. Let your Kingdom come, let your will be done.

A DECREE

From my position in Christ at God's own right hand, I decree that I am loosed from the power and influence of the devil. I decree that all deaf and dumb spirits must go and all spirits of spiritual blindness must go. I loose myself from all doctrinal error and all teaching that would hinder and block my relationship with God. I call for God's light to fill me to overflowing and dispel all darkness. I declare that I am light just like my Heavenly Father. I receive everything that the Lord has for me without reservation.

CONTENTS

TO THOSE WITH FAITH, NO EXPLANATION IS NECESSSARY
TO THOSE WITHOUT FAITH, NO EXPLANATION IS POSSIBLE

ST. THOMAS AQUINAS

1

BUILDING ON A FIRM FOUNDATION

As we pursue and learn about translation by faith, or anything of the Kingdom really, it's very important the we be grounded in the Word of God and have a firm foundation. There are core beliefs and truths that keep us anchored as we move deeper into the "meat" of the scriptures.

Unlike merely learning to memorize scripture or learning about the history of Bible characters, learning about the supernatural things of God presents a bit of a greater challenge. Because the church in general has had very little instruction about such things, we must have a "Plumb line" to keep us true. The plumb line we have is of course the Word of God, but it is also the inward witness of the Holy Spirit and the testimony of saints who have lived lives unto God with fruit to prove it.

Having a solid salvation, a solid understanding of the word and a solid commitment to Christ, gives us the foundation to pursue the supernatural things of the Bible with fearless confidence and assurance as we stay in God's will. If our motivation is Christ, it leaves very little room for error and deception from the enemy.

We cannot teach the supernatural things of God without making clear those requirements that we must embrace to make us like a rock, anchored to *the* rock, the Lord Jesus Christ.

Salvation

1 There was a man of the Pharisees, named Nicodemus, a ruler of the Jews:

2 The same came to Jesus by night, and said unto him, Rabbi, we know that thou art a teacher come from God: for no man can do these miracles that thou doest, except God be with him.

3 Jesus answered and said unto him, Verily, verily, I say unto thee, Except a man be born again, he cannot see the kingdom of God.

4 Nicodemus saith unto him, How can a man be born when he is old? can he enter the second time into his mother's womb, and be born?

5 Jesus answered, Verily, verily, I say unto thee, Except a man be born of water and of the Spirit, he cannot enter into the kingdom of God.

6 That which is born of the flesh is flesh; and that which is born of the Spirit is spirit.

7 Marvel not that I said unto thee, Ye must be born again. (John 3:1-7)

You must be born again.

Being born again not only gives us a relationship with God, salvation and the benefits that come from that relationship, but the Holy Spirit who leads us in all truth. Being born again is not just saying some "magic words" like many have believed it to be. There is a turning from our sin, in recognition of what Christ has done for us by giving His life on the cross. We repent of our sins and that lifestyle of following the world and turn to follow Christ, leaving the old life behind.

Salvation is being born of the spirit....becoming one spirit with God...Becoming a new creation in Christ.

Therefore, if any man be in Christ, he is a new creature: old things are passed away; behold, all things are become new. (2Corinthians 5:17)

The old desires become dead to us. The fleshly nature is put to death. You literally become a new creature. There is a great reality and mystery here. The reason that we can do the things that Christ has instructed us to do is because of the fact that we are now sons of God.

But as many as received him, to them gave he power to become the sons of God, even to them that believe on his name: (John 1:12)

The Baptism of the Holy Spirit

What empowers believers to be able to live for God in a world that is anti-Christ? The infilling of the Holy Spirit. The power of God resident in us gives us the power we need to live for God *and* to do the works that we have been commanded to do, such as those things mentioned in Matthew chapter ten.

Heal the sick, cleanse the lepers, raise the dead, cast out devils: freely ye have received, freely give. (Matthew 10:8)

The things that we have been commanded to do are impossible to do without Him. We are completely dependent upon the Lord to empower us for the lives we are called to live.

And, behold, I send the promise of my Father upon you: but tarry ye in the city of Jerusalem, until ye be endued with power from on high. (Luke 24:49)

Pursuing the supernatural things of God is possible only because of the Holy Spirit.

He gives us assurance that we are going in the right direction. We can trust the Holy Spirit. It is His job to give us instruction in the things of God.

Howbeit when he, the Spirit of truth, is come, he will guide you into all truth: for he shall not speak of himself; but whatsoever he shall hear, that shall he speak: and he will shew you things to come. (John 16:13)

Praying / Speaking in Tongues

I thank God that I speak in tongues more than all of you. (1 Corinthians 14:18)

There has to be a reason that Paul would say this and a reason that the Holy Spirit wants us to know it by placing it in scripture. Let's look at some compelling reasons.

The Lord Gave This to Us.

How foolish would it be, to be given a gift or an empowerment from God and then deem it unnecessary to pursue or accept or walk in? If for no other reason than it has been given us by God we should receive it.

In Luke twenty-four, we have been told that they have been instructed to wait for the empowerment of the Holy Spirit. This shows the importance of it. We are also told that after they were filled they spoke with other tongues.

And they were all filled with the Holy Ghost, and began to speak with other tongues, as the Spirit gave them utterance. (Acts 2:4)

Build up Your Spirit

These are the people who divide you, who follow mere natural instincts and do not have the Spirit. But ye, beloved, building up yourselves on your most holy faith, praying in the Holy Ghost, (Jude 1:19-20)

I included the verse nineteen also from Jude chapter one for a good reason. When you do not have the Holy Spirit and His power and leading in your life, the best you can do is rely on your natural reasoning....your natural instincts. This is where most people run into trouble. This is what provides us with the powerless "gospel" that we are warned about in second Timothy.

*But know this, that in the last days perilous times will come: 2 For men will be lovers of themselves, lovers of money, boasters, proud, blasphemers, disobedient to parents, unthankful, unholy, 3 unloving, unforgiving, slanderers, without self-control, brutal, despisers of good, 4 traitors, headstrong, haughty, lovers of pleasure rather than lovers of God, 5 **having a form of godliness but denying its power. And from such people turn away!** 6 For of this sort are those who creep into households and make captives of gullible women loaded down with sins, led away by various lusts, 7 **always learning and never able to come to the knowledge of the truth.** (2Timothy 3:1-7)*

Does this mean that all of those people who are in these religious churches are wicked? No, of course not, but it does mean that they are in deception to one degree or another. The Gospel of Jesus Christ is not something that needs to be improved upon with religious trappings and rules and rituals. Those types of things satisfy the flesh, not the Spirit. The Lord Jesus made this clear all throughout His ministry, especially in His dealings with the Pharisees. In *Luke chapter eleven* Jesus talks about observing the rules but ignoring the real issues.

We are building ourselves up when we pray in tongues, or speak in tongues. If you spend any amount of time at all praying in tongues, you can literally feel the difference as the Holy Spirit builds you up. Your faith becomes stronger, the fruit of the Spirit becomes more evident and natural in your life and the gifts of the Spirit flow more powerfully.

By yielding your tongue, which is the "rudder" of your being, you are yielding yourself to the Holy Spirit and allowing Him to do the works within you that need to be done.

Passion for Christ

Ask any Godly person who flows powerfully in the supernatural things of God, and they will tell you that the "key" is the relationship with The Lord Jesus. The closer we get to him, all the other things become manifest. When you hear certain ministers teach and they focus so heavily on our relationship with Christ you may wonder *"When are they going to start teaching about angels or healing or Heaven?"* The reason is because we have to be connected and grounded firmly in our relationship with Christ and in the Word. God will not pour His power through an unyielding or an un-yielded vessel no matter how much we might desire it.

Our reason must be Christ. Our desire and our focus and our life must be Christ.

To whom God would make known what is the riches of the glory of this mystery among the Gentiles; which is Christ in you, the hope of glory: (Colossians 1:27)

Frankly, if you are not sold out to Him, you will not have fellowship with the things of Heaven. The common bond is Jesus Christ. Angels will enjoy being around you if you are in Love with Him. If you worship Him and live for Him, you have something in common with the angels. (And the saints etc.)

If we only pursue the supernatural things of God without the relationship, we are already in deception.

Christ-Like Character

If I had to pick one key to really moving in the power of God and the supernatural, it would be "Christ-like character."

You see the revelation and awareness and the coming together of our heart with His happens as we start to become more like Jesus. As we become more like Him, we will do the things He does. What did Jesus say about what He does?

Then answered Jesus and said unto them, Verily, verily, I say unto you, The Son can do nothing of himself, but what he seeth the Father do: for what things soever he doeth, these also doeth the Son likewise. (John 5:19)

As we become more like Him, our understanding becomes that we do only those things that are pleasing to Him...those things that we see Him do. This is not about what we would like to do or where we would like to go. It is *"What is the Father saying?"* Those are the things that I will do.

We see a powerful picture of this in the life of Enoch. In Genesis chapter five we learn something very telling about what it takes to move in the supernatural of God.

And Enoch walked with God: and he was not; for God took him. (Genesis 5:24)

Enoch was so fused together with the character of God that when people looked at him what they saw was God. His character was such that he moved and behaved and appeared as a mature son of God. That's the place we need to be in. If you have never read the testimony of Enoch, you should. Recorded in the Book of Enoch is a record of how the Lord taught him about the things of Heaven. (The book of Enoch is quoted throughout the Bible) Enoch had incredible experiences in God. He was shown angelic hierarchies and the four corners of the Earth. He walked in the stars and in the Heavens and saw the gates of Heaven. Enoch walked in the Spirit.

We can be encouraged by his testimony to pursue that same kind of relationship with God. Enoch has a powerful testimony and his work for the Kingdom is far from over. Those who are forerunners in this thing called translation by faith, know this well.

Christ-like character is walking in the fruit of the Spirit.

I say then: Walk in the Spirit, and you shall not fulfill the lust of the flesh. 17 For the flesh lusts against the Spirit, and the Spirit against the flesh; and these are contrary to one another, so that you do not do the things that you wish. 18 But if you are led by the

Spirit, you are not under the law. 19 Now the works of the flesh are evident, which are: adultery,[c] fornication, uncleanness, lewdness, 20 idolatry, sorcery, hatred, contentions, jealousies, outbursts of wrath, selfish ambitions, dissensions, heresies, 21 envy, murders,[d] drunkenness, revelries, and the like; of which I tell you beforehand, just as I also told you in time past, that those who practice such things will not inherit the kingdom of God. 22 But the fruit of the Spirit is love, joy, peace, longsuffering, kindness, goodness, faithfulness, 23 gentleness, self-control. Against such there is no law. 24 And those who are Christ's have crucified the flesh with its passions and desires. 25 If we live in the Spirit, let us also walk in the Spirit. (Galatians 5:16-25)

Christ-likeness is our goal. It is spiritual growth manifested. The fruit of the spirit is the perfect picture of Christ-likeness for us. As these things become more evident in our lives, we are becoming more like Him.

... till we all come to the unity of the faith and of the knowledge of the Son of God, to a perfect man, to the measure of the stature of the fullness of Christ; 14 that we should no longer be children, tossed to and fro and carried about with every wind of doctrine, by the trickery of men, in the cunning craftiness of deceitful plotting, 15 but, speaking the truth in love, may grow up in all things into Him who is the head—Christ— 16 from whom the whole body, joined and knit together by what every joint supplies, according to the effective working by which every part does its share, causes growth of the body for the edifying of itself in love. (Ephesians 4:13-16)

To walk in the power or the gifts of the Spirit, you must be walking in the fruit of the Spirit as well.

God is much more concerned about your character and your relationship with Him than He is about any gifts, or anointings, or callings. He cares more about the condition of your soul than whether you are doing great works for the Kingdom. That is what any good Father or parent would focus on.

Keep short accounts. Ask the Holy Spirit to search you on a regular basis and expose anything that offends Him or defiles you. Let this be the thing that you are aware of, that you are always well pleasing to God. If you will do this, you can walk in the supernatural power of God.

Avoiding Deception

This is a necessary topic to discuss for many reasons. The enemy does not want you to walk in the power of God. He does not want you to see the unseen or walk in the supernatural in any way, shape, or form. If your eyes are open, it is harder for the enemy to deceive you. If you have knowledge and understanding about supernatural things, the enemy can't lead you astray as he would someone who is ignorant about these things.

We have to be sober and vigilant about our walk in Christ.

Be sober, be vigilant; because your adversary the devil, as a roaring lion, walketh about, seeking whom he may devour: (1 Peter 5:8)

Lest Satan should get an advantage of us: for we are not ignorant of his devices. (2 Corinthians 2:11)

Especially concerning spiritual gifts and manifestations, the enemy wants us to be uncertain or confused. This is why there is so much disagreement about such things in the body today. But our goal is not to appease people or compromise so that people will like us or so that our "ministry" can grow. Our only goal and aim is to do the will of Him who sent you. Of course we walk in love as we do this because we are trying to win others to Christ, but we do not compromise the truth.

Source Matters

I read a book not too long ago about holiness that asked an important question. "*Just how much defilement is acceptable to us?*" Seems like a strange question until we begin to apply it to our own lives and circumstances.

If I gave you a glass of water to drink and by all appearances it looked crystal clear and clean, but I told you that it had zero point five percent of waste in it, would you want to drink it? Of course not. What if the water was clean but the glass had been previously filled with waste and then not cleaned, would that be ok? No it wouldn't. We all understand that.

This brings us to consider the source when learning about the supernatural things of God.

The Spirit of Truth

<u>The Holy Spirit is the one who leads us into all truth</u>. Period

There are many groups and religions and doctrines, that talk about the same things that we talk about. Many new age gurus talk about healing and seeing the unseen and such things including moving supernaturally. We just have to know that. There is the true gift and manifestation given by God and there is the counterfeit.

It is not surprising to me that people who walk in the counterfeit spiritual things have some real and true knowledge. The enemy has always been very effective at mixing things to deceive those who are not aware. The enemy takes a truth and defiles it in some small and imperceptible way.... Just like the drinking water.

When someone who is not led by the spirit of God shares a truth with you, if you receive it you are also receiving a part of the source of that revelation. A bit of defilement as it were.

Many people never even know that they have been defiled. Those who share their "knowledge" may not even be aware that they are doing a work for the enemy.

This is a very real problem today. Because so few Christians walk in the supernatural and so few Churches teach about it, many who are seeking have come to believe that it's ok to learn from other sources as long as the information is helpful and correct. They believe that as long as they use that information or revelation for good, or for the Kingdom of God, that makes it ok.

There is no provision for this or precedent for this in the Word. This is a danger that leads to bondage. Always seek God for revelation. Always.

Two things... Follow Jesus and be a student of the Word.

2

GET UNDERSTANDING

What is Translation by Faith?

In its simplest explanation, translation by faith is moving supernaturally by the Spirit of God for His purposes. Translation means to be "caught away." Many also call this translocation or transportation. For our purposes to make things clear and to distinguish the spiritual phenomenon from the natural, we will refer to the spiritual catching away as translation and the physical catching away as translocation.

The spiritual and or physical aspect can look like this...

It is doubtless not profitable for me to boast. I will come to visions and revelations of the Lord: 2 I know a man in Christ who fourteen years ago—whether in the body I do not know, or whether out of the body I do not know, God knows—such a one was caught up to the third heaven. 3 And I know such a man—whether in the body or out of the body I do not know, God knows— 4 how he was caught up into Paradise and heard inexpressible words, which it is not lawful for a man to utter. 5 Of such a one I will boast; yet of myself I will not boast, except in my infirmities. 6 For though I might desire to boast, I will not be a fool ; for I will speak the truth. But I refrain, lest anyone should think of me above what he sees me to be or hears from me. (2 Corinthians 12:1-6)

Very often, when engaging the realm of the spirit, it is very hard to tell whether you are experiencing things solely in the spirit or if your body is also involved. The overwhelming power and awareness of your spirit man can make it seem as if you are still functioning in your physical body even if you are not. Thus Paul's explanation that "whether in the body or out of the body, I do not know..."

The physical aspect can look like this...

26 Now an angel of the Lord spoke to Philip, saying, "Arise and go toward the south along the road which goes down from Jerusalem to Gaza." This is desert. 27 So he arose and went. And behold, a man of Ethiopia, a eunuch of great authority under Candace the queen of the Ethiopians, who had charge of all her treasury, and had come to Jerusalem to worship, 28 was returning. And sitting in his chariot, he was reading Isaiah the prophet. 29 Then the Spirit said to Philip, "Go near and overtake this chariot." 30 So Philip ran to him, and heard him reading the prophet Isaiah, and said, "Do you understand what you are reading?" 31 And he said, "How can I, unless someone guides me?" And he asked Philip to come up and sit with him. 32 The place in the Scripture which he read was this:

"He was led as a sheep to the slaughter;

And as a lamb before its shearer is silent,

So He opened not His mouth.33

In His humiliation His justice was taken away,

And who will declare His generation?

For His life is taken from the earth."[b]

34 So the eunuch answered Philip and said, "I ask you, of whom does the prophet say this, of himself or of some other man?" 35 Then Philip opened his mouth, and beginning at this Scripture, preached Jesus to him. 36 Now as they went down the road, they came to some water. And the eunuch said, "See, here is water. What hinders me from being baptized?" 37 Then Philip said, "If you believe with all your heart, you may."

And he answered and said, "I believe that Jesus Christ is the Son of God."

38 So he commanded the chariot to stand still. And both Philip and the eunuch went down into the water, and he baptized him. 39 Now when they came up out of the water, the Spirit of the Lord caught Philip away, so that the eunuch saw him no more; and he went on his way rejoicing. 40 But Philip was found at Azotus. And passing through, he preached in all the cities till he came to Caesarea. (Acts 8:26-40)

In keeping with our explanation that these events in the life of a believer are for the purposes of God, we see in verse 26 that an angel set Philip on this journey he was about to undertake. It also shows that Philip was obedient because he arose and went. Through this particular encounter we are learning a few things about these types of experiences. We can also see that the Holy Spirit told him to "go near and overtake the chariot" but it doesn't say that God gave him the whole picture before Philip decided to obey God. That is something to keep in mind. God often gives us the next step, but rarely tells us everything in advance. That is where the "by faith" comes in. Learning to hear and discern the voice of God is part of moving in the supernatural of God.

The spiritual aspect can look like this...

I, John, both your brother and companion in the tribulation and kingdom and patience of Jesus Christ, was on the island that is called Patmos for the word of God and for the testimony of Jesus Christ. 10 I was in the Spirit on the Lord's Day, and I heard behind me a loud voice, as of a trumpet, 11 saying, "I am the Alpha and the Omega, the First and the Last," and "What you see, write in a book and send it to the seven churches which are in Asia; to Ephesus, to Smyrna, to Pergamos, to Thyatira, to Sardis, to Philadelphia, and to Laodicea." (Revelation 1:9-11)

Here John says clearly that he was in the spirit on the Lord's day. He obviously knew it and also experienced many things and recorded them according to what he was told to do. One thing we can learn from this encounter in the spiritual realm is that John is experiencing all kinds of revelation and encountering many things but has clarity to interact and function in that realm.

Things experienced in the spiritual realm seem very normal when you are in that realm. Things that you think might really challenge you such as virtually the entire book of Revelation that John experienced seem more normal when you are in the spirit.

There are many examples in the Bible of people moving supernaturally by the Spirit of God. Name all that you can think of or find and whether they are physical, spiritual or both. (+ Script. Ref.)

Gleaning Some Exciting Truths

From all of the examples we looked at and also from those that you found in the Word, we can see some things that are very encouraging. First, we see that God has done this time and again throughout the history of our faith. This is not some isolated incident that we are trying to pretend is something more. God does this! Secondly, we see that God has used many different people in this way. John, Philip, Elijah, Ezekiel, The Lord Jesus, Paul, as well as others have experienced this.

Why should you be excited about this? Because God is no respecter of persons! What He has done for one of His, He will do for another. That means you! (Acts 10:34)

Also, we see that God is using people who are sold out to Him. There doesn't seem to be any other qualification that has to be met to walk in this. You as someone who is sold out to God have been qualified by Christ and are in position to walk in this. How do I know that you are sold out? Just by virtue of the fact that you are reading this book or attending the school shows that you are not trying to fulfill the religious minimum.

We can also see that God makes it easy if we just obey His voice. You don't have to know every step in advance, you just have to be willing to take that next step as God reveals it.

Has God Done This in the Past and Why?

List the scripture references of your examples and what God's purpose was in doing this.

Why Would God do This Today?

Here is a question that throws a lot of people. Why would God do things like this today? It seems like a logical question. We have communication devices that connect us instantly with the other side of the world. We have natural transportation like cars and trains and aircraft that can take us pretty much anywhere in the world quickly. God doesn't really need to do it this way anymore because we are so advanced, right?

Before we explore this, please take some time and list serious reasons why you think God would still do this today. What kinds of scenarios would warrant supernatural transportations and translations? How does the world we live in, advanced or not play a part? Do Christians need this? Will Christians need this? And why?

Give Six Good Reasons

The thing to remember about God doing the supernatural is that it is in no way contingent upon this worlds systems or advances or beliefs etc.. Although the examples are not as extreme in nature, God could have allowed Philip to ride a horse to get him from the baptism of the Eunuch to Azotus, the city to which he was transported..

When Elijah was moved supernaturally by a chariot of fire, God could have done it in any number of ways to appease unbelievers but He did not. God is a supernatural God, a Spirit (John 4:24) and He knows the end from the beginning. He didn't work Himself into the parameters of natural life and living where he could. He is God. God does the supernatural because that is who He is. Jesus still heals today and the fact that we have "advanced" medical facilities doesn't even enter into the equation.

And it came to pass, as they still went on, and talked, that, behold, there appeared a chariot of fire, and horses of fire, and separated them both; and Elijah went up by a whirlwind into heaven. (2 Kings 2:11)

Some Clarity and Explanation

In Hebrews 13:8 it says.. Jesus Christ is the same yesterday and today and forever.

God does not change with the times no matter how much that many in the "church" of today would like to believe it. God has always done the supernatural. Miracles, signs and wonders are normal for Him and for His children. (us) The church of recent history in general has been pretty much a powerless form of godliness. It's not that we don't love the Lord. The problem is we have taken someone's word for something we should be talking to the Lord directly about. We have been taught that all the "God" stuff was for a different time and that's why we don't see it today. It becomes a handy excuse to live our own lives instead of pressing in for God and all that He has for us.

God Never Stopped

God always has a remnant. There have always been people whose entire existence is all about God. If we examine for a moment the lives of the remnant of people who continued to walk in the supernatural over the past few hundred years we can see that all of the Biblical accounts have been repeated and reproduced by God over and over including supernatural translations and transportations.

St Joseph of Cupertino (1603-1663) is one of the Saints who is best known for levitating during prayer . He was often carried away by God for some distance. In the records of his life, seventy of his levitations and flights are recorded.

St Gerard Majella (1726-1755) was often taken into remarkable levitations, often being moved by God for great distances. On one occasion, two of his companions watched him rise into the air and fly with the speed of a bird to a distance of almost a mile. After seeing this, they would often retell of this amazing event of which they had been witnesses.

Saint Martin de Porres (1579-1639) He could fly through the air, as well as bi-locate.

Reliable eye witnesses have testified that Saint Martin de Porres had been seen doing missionary work in Asia and in Mexico, even though he never left Lima, Peru.

Saint Francis Xavier (1506-1552)The reason he was so successful in his efforts of evangelism is because he was reportedly able to be in multiple places at the same time. These bi-locations St. Francis experienced happened very frequently and were seen and documented by many eye witnesses.

St. (Padre) Pio (1887-1968) God graced Padre Pio with many extraordinary spiritual gifts. Among them, the gifts of healing, tongues, bi-location, working of miracles and the ability to see and work with angels. Despite the gifts he never put the gifts before the giver and always remained humble concerning them.

There are many, many more in Christ who moved supernaturally for the Kingdom. It is interesting to read the histories of some of these men and women of God. Doing so can inspire you as you lay hold of this yourself.

Present Day Manifestations

The few that were just mentioned are some of the very well-known people from the church history but it didn't stop with them either. God continues to be God and continues to translate and transport his own supernaturally for His plans and purposes.

Brother Grubbs (1913-2009) over a span of about thirty years, Brother Grubbs, a Pentecostal pastor was transported supernaturally all over the world to preach and pray and minister for the Lord. He would also bring back little gifts for his wife when the Lord would take him to foreign lands.

John Paul Jackson (1950-2015) an author and minister of the Gospel who was well known in the prophetic arena, teaching much about dreams and visions gave an incredible testimony concerning supernatural translocation. While John Paul was in the hospital, suddenly a very old Hispanic man materialized by his bedside, The man prayed for him then vanished. John Paul said he knew it wasn't an angel and he asked the Lord who it was. The Lord told him that this man passionately desired to be used of God but lived in an isolated place and had no ability to travel. The Lord had honored his desire and transported him and used him.

Dr. James Maloney (-present) respected prophetic minister for over 40 years and moves in incredible healings, signs and wonders recently recounted an experience where the Lord Jesus physically transported him to an Eastern European nation, where the Lord and Dr. Maloney prayed for a massive throng of people seeing incredible healings that astonished the crowd. When Dr. Maloney was transported back home he was still covered in the dust and dirt of the area , clothes and shoes.

This is only three of the modern day examples, but there are many, many more. This is becoming an ever increasing phenomenon with literally new testimonies every day.

Jesus is Looking For Volunteers

We look at the lives of the saints of old and its easy for us to understand why God would use these people. They appear larger than life to us. People like John, Enoch, Ezekiel and Moses, are heroes to us. We are supposed to honor those who have gone before us. That's ok, but we are not supposed to put them on a pedestal. If we put a distance between us and those of the faith who in reality are actually of our own family, we create a barrier that makes it hard for us to follow their example or their directions. (by the Holy Spirit) This placing a "respectful distance" between us and them is both popular and unbiblical. God did not call certain special people to do the important stuff and too bad for everyone else. No. God specializes in using the foolish things to confound the wise. He takes a person that no one would suspect could do incredible things and then does incredible things through them. Why? Because this way God receives all the glory!

The Lord wants to use you and me. He desires to give us wonderful assignments like the saints of old. Many in the church today have the ungodly idea that we are somehow not worthy to have that close, face to face, over the top, supernatural relationship with God and this wrong thinking keeps many people from fulfilling their God-given destiny. The scripture is where we look for the truth. Forget anything that anyone tells you that is contrary to scripture.

The Law of First Mention

As we seek to discover who we are in Christ and what really belongs to us, there is something called the law of first mention that breaks open for us what the scriptures are saying, when we have questions as to what pertains to us really any question where we need clarification on the word. The law of first mention is this... when something is mentioned in the Bible for the first time, from that point on you can use that first mention as a base point to interpret all other scriptures that speak of the same subject.

Let's take a look at an example. The scripture says in Genesis 1:26-31 that man was created on the sixth day. So from that point on we understand that six is the number of man. Anytime you see the word man or the number six, you can know that it's talking about flesh or man. This is the law of first mention.

Also in Genesis we find Jacob sleeping and meditating in the night season upon God. During the night, it says he had a dream that profoundly changed his life. He saw a ladder going from Earth to Heaven with the angels of God ascending and descending upon it. This is important and we need to understand this. Man was made from the dust of the Earth This ladder begins on the Earth and extends into Heaven. He sees this ladder and the angels of God are ascending and descending upon it, and at the top of this ladder he saw the Lord and he talked with Him face to face.

When Jacob woke up the next morning he made a statement...a first mention. :...This is none other than the house of God, and this is the gateway of Heaven."(Gen. 28:17) How does this apply to us? First Corinthians says, Or do you not know that your body is the temple of the Holy Spirit who is in you, whom you have from God, and you are not your own? (1 Corinthians 6:19)

What is the principle that we can gleam from that first mention? It is this... The house of God is the gateway of Heaven and you are the temple or the house of God. The angels are seen ascending and descending upon this house and conversation with the Lord is face to face. That is what we were created for!

According to the law of first mention, we as the temples of God are to be continually walking under an open Heaven, talking to Him face to face and seeing angelic activity!

A Spectacular Revelation

Because of the law of first mention we can realize that all of the amazing things of the Bible belong to us. For instance, based on the law of first mention there is a scripture in Genesis (a first mention) that is life changing and exactly the kind of example we need to help propel us into the supernatural things of God.

The very first mention of a relationship with God is walking and talking with Him face to face each day. (Gen. 3:8) That is the correct picture of a relationship with God! We should be walking and talking with Him face to face! There are many first mentions in the Bible that let us know what our relationship with God should be. We can ask the Holy Spirit to show us in the Word these first mentions and then walk in that reality. You see, it isn't just Moses that could speak to God face to face as a friend, but you can too. All of the amazing promises of the Bible are yours. God has you to pour His love and His power through. You are qualified through Christ. All of these scriptures pertain to you and belong to you.

God's Covenants: Who Are You and What belongs to you?

List some scriptures that support our assertion that show you are qualified to an intimate, supernatural and powerful relationship with God.

** Take your time and find the scriptures that really speak to you. Find the ones that touch your heart and cause you to be able to believe that God can and will use you in the most amazing ways. Find those promises that speak about or relate to this subject.

A Prayer

Dear Lord, Show me your ways. Teach me about this translation by faith and use me in this way for your glory. I yield myself completely and totally to your will, your purpose and your plans and I am willing to go where you tell me to go and do what you tell me to do. Give me revelation, wisdom and understanding. Teach me more every day and let this be my normal, everyday reality. In Christ's name, Amen.

Exercises of Spiritual Engagement

As we begin to engage this spiritual reality we will use spiritual "gateways" or "access points." Don't let the terminology throw you. Spiritual access points are things like prayer, worship, meditating on the Lord or His word and "being still" and knowing I am God. They can also be specific places. The exercises that are forthcoming may seem very simple to some but you cannot measure the full weight of these exercises until you have laid hold of them, done them and tasted the fruit of them. These exercises of engaging with God will take you to a relationship with God beyond what you have ever known.

Eph 2: 6 "And He raised us up with Him and seated us with Him in the heavenly places in Mesiah Yeshua

Engagement

Choose a scripture that you really like that in some way talks about translation or transportation by faith. Find a quiet and comfortable place to sit , away from distractions if possible and read through the passage.

Now read through the passage again, and after each verse, close your eyes and visualize the scene in your imagination. Just the way you might if someone asked you to remember a nice vacation that you once had. Be calm and relaxed and look at the "pictures" that each verse inspires.

Now read through the passage again and visualize the entire passage again. Do this many times and try to really "see" with your imagination the clothing, the weather, the sights and sounds and smells and fragrances of the scene.

Do this many times. An hour is a good starting point for an exercise like this if you desire to makes significant strides in using this simple but effective entry point.

Engagement

Again, find a quiet and comfortable place to pray and engage the Lord. Close your eyes and "see" the Lord's face. Meditate on his face, or what you believe he might look like. Look at his features. Look into his eyes. Look at the light that comes from him. Feel his light upon you as you look at him.

Do this also for one hour. For some this may be a little difficult, but it gets easier. As we experience the Lord's presence in these exercises, it gets much, much easier!

**These exercises will be explained more fully in an upcoming section with reasons and explanations given so that you have a complete understanding with scriptural references to establish them.

**When we talk about engaging the imagination, we begin to see why it's important to know the true meanings of the scriptures from the original languages.

3

BIBLICAL SUPERNATURAL

Establishing a Baseline

As we seek to embrace the things of God, many times there are religious objections that come up in our minds that cause us to have doubt and unbelief. Because the majority of the church in recent history has not only disbelieved the supernatural things of God but have also distained and denigrated them, often attributing the mighty works of God to the devil, many of us are afflicted by those ungodly doctrines of demons and men. (Matthew 15:9) No I'm not saying that the men who say these things are purposely trying to mislead people, but what often happens is preachers will often accept the explanations of other preachers they deem to be wise and Godly without getting the revelation for themselves. The end result can be generations of people who truly love God but are preaching a wrong doctrine or theology.

Or... it can also mean that people can get filled up with religious pride and sometimes relentlessly attack those who do believe that things like miracles, healings and angels are for today. There seems to be a lot of those kind of people as well.

Let them alone: they be blind leaders of the blind. And if the blind lead the blind, both shall fall into the ditch. (Matthew 15:14)

Unfortunately, this very thing has happened concerning the supernatural things of God. The first century church that moved in such awesome displays of the power of God is not the same church we see today. (for the most part) As we pursue translation by faith, it is important that all of the incorrect interpretations of the Word and the ungodly explanations are shattered so that they never cause us trouble or hold us back as we go all out for God. Our God is a supernatural God.

Manifestations of God's Power

Most of the people going through this workbook I would think have already decided in themselves that God still does the miraculous. (Malachi 3:6) That's probably why you are reading this book.

Many people have heard of signs and wonders that are sometimes difficult to believe. Are there any that challenge you? Are there scriptures that we could use to validate or dismiss them? If you are in a group, discuss this.

What are your scripture references? Are there any scriptures that cast doubt on your belief? Again be thorough. As you are breaking new ground, many of you forerunners in this reality, you may be asked to give an answer or explanation. Many times our friends and families have no understanding and have not been taught about these things.

If you filled in the list above, you probably wrote down things like healings, deliverance, angelic visitations, supernatural provision, translation by faith, ascending into the Heavens and other things as well. Are there any scriptures in the Bible that would cause you to believe that maybe God doesn't do this anymore? Any scriptures that cause you to think that you would have to be someone important in the "church world" to be used of God? Can you find a scripture that says God stopped healing or helping etc.?

There is no point in wasting space with more lines. The truth is that there are none, but a couple of scriptures are always presented by the naysayers who claim that God no longer does the miraculous. One of them is 1 Corinthians 13:10. Here is what it says...

But when that which is perfect is come, then that which is in part shall be done away. (1 Corinthians 13:10)

The reasoning or argument is that because we have the Holy Bible, that all of the spiritual gifts and supernatural manifestations of God have been done away with. Those that believe this believe that "the perfect" is the Bible.

Charity never faileth: but whether there be prophecies, they shall fail; whether there be tongues, they shall cease; whether there be knowledge, it shall vanish away. For we know in part, and we prophesy in part. But when that which is perfect is come, then that which is in part shall be done away. (1 Corinthians 13:8-10)

The church at large for many years had very few moving in the power of God. They had to come up with a reason why no one was getting healed or delivered in their churches. Why were there no miraculous happenings in their churches? This scripture in Corinthians was the handiest explanation. If you look at this example you realize that you must really stretch yourself to believe it says what many claim it does. To say that which is perfect is the Bible is incredibly erroneous because even though the Bible is the best- selling book period, there are countless millions throughout the world who don't even have a Bible. On top of that, the Bible as we know it didn't even exist until 1455 and they were printed one at a time. Just from an examination of the timeline we see it makes no sense. Also, this scripture mentions tongues, prophecy and knowledge.

The dis-believers also throw in healings and all the rest using the same convoluted reasoning. This is a doctrine of demons meant to keep the power of God and the supernatural things of God out of the church and out of the believers. The devil doesn't mind you going to church or really even if you read the Bible. What he will fight tooth and nail is the supernatural power of God, the manifestation of the Holy Spirit in our lives.

Christ is the Perfect

Jesus Christ is the perfect spoken of in that scripture. When Jesus is come, there will be no need for partial prophecy or incomplete knowledge or tongues.

Beloved, now are we the sons of God, and it doth not yet appear what we shall be: but we know that, when he shall appear, we shall be like him; for we shall see him as he is. (1 John 3:2)

Notice the highlighted part. We shall be like Him. There will be no need for anything partial or imperfect working in us because we will be like Him. Complete.

Settle This Within Yourself

So until the day that we see Him face to face and we shall be like Him, we operate through the gifts of the Holy Spirit. The importance of settling this is that as you lay hold of translation by faith, the enemy will bring people into your path to try to dissuade you and discourage you. They will tell you that God doesn't do those things. They don't even have to get you to actually believe it. All the enemy has to do is discourage you enough that doubt is sown so as to derail your pursuit of God. Which brings us to another reality....

Surround Yourself With Like-Minded Believers

Be ye not unequally yoked together with unbelievers: for what fellowship hath righteousness with unrighteousness? and what communion hath light with darkness? (2 Corinthians 6:14)

This scripture may be speaking of fellowship with those who do not accept Jesus as Savior and Lord, but it also is wise counsel for fellowship concerning those who embrace Jesus but deny the Holy Spirit and His work.

There is safety in wise counsel. (Proverbs 11:14) There is power in agreement.

Again I say unto you, That if two of you shall agree on earth as touching any thing that they shall ask, it shall be done for them of my Father which is in heaven. (Matthew 18:19)

The problem with fellowship with those who don't believe in God's power today is that there really is no agreement at all. Yes, people will be civil sometimes and you can have superficial conversations about the Lord but in general those who do not believe the supernatural of God is for today rarely even believe people like us who do are even saved. That is the reality. We can't sugar-coat this because the stakes are too high.

That is one of the "wonderful" things about manifesting the love of God to people. Even though they may not agree with you there will always be one or two who are willing to take you aside and tell you that everyone really thinks you are nuts. It happens so expect it.

Surround yourself with those who are pressing into God with a passion that seems foolish to the world. Make friends with those who are sold out and have made their decision. Then as you pray together there will be genuine agreement and the heavens will move on your behalf. There is a bond that we have that goes beyond family.

When you pray with these fellow lovers of God you will experience breakthrough and the gifts that flow through you and them will be manifest on your behalf and great advances will be made in the spiritual realm. That is the way God designed it.

As iron sharpens iron, So a man sharpens the countenance of his friend. (Proverbs 27:17)

.If your fellowship is with the worldly, they will pull you down to their comfort level.

A little leaven leaveneth the whole lump. (Galatians 5:9)

Words are Powerful Things

In the beginning God spoke and a creative force was released and everything came into being. We are sons and daughters of God who are created in His likeness. Things happen when we speak. We need to be aware of that. In addition to the supernatural aspect of words and speaking them (or releasing sounds and Heavenly frequencies-worship is an example) there is the natural aspect that also plays a very key part.

In coming to the conclusion that biblical and supernatural are not mutually exclusive terms, we have to realize and acknowledge that the meanings of the words and their contexts as well as the cultural influence and the mindset of the culture all play a part.

The scripture was written by God through men who described things according to their own points of knowledge and reference. God did not cause these men to write in English according to what twenty-first century western society would believe or embrace.

Understand by the Spirit

When people begin to "understand" words or instructions from the Bible according to their own natural understanding, we begin to get into trouble. In the modern day church the tendency has been to take supernatural words and passages and events in the scripture and try to remake them or explain them as natural.

This is one reason why I encourage you to do word studies in the passages that you are studying. Get into the original Greek and Hebrew meanings for those passages and see what God is really saying rather than just taking someone else's word and hoping they are right. Correct understanding is a key to unlock the supernatural of God for you.

In the Name of Jesus

This has not been only a modern day phenomenon though. Even during the times of the first century church, we see powerful examples of misinterpretation. Take for instance the seven sons of Sceva

Some Jews who went around driving out evil spirits tried to invoke the name of the Lord Jesus over those who were demon-possessed. They would say, "In the name of the Jesus whom Paul preaches, I command you to come out." Seven sons of Sceva, a Jewish chief priest, were doing this. One day the evil spirit answered them, "Jesus I know, and Paul I know about, but who are you?" Then the man who had the evil spirit jumped on them and overpowered them all. He gave them such a beating that they ran out of the house naked and bleeding. (Acts 19:13-16)

They had the idea that if they said the right words, the evil spirits would have to obey them. "In the name of Jesus" were those words and for them the words had no power. They had no understanding in this matter. We have the exact same problem today.

Many today pray or declare something "in the name of Jesus" and wonder why it doesn't' work. Here again, understanding brings it into the light.

John 14:13 says this,

Whatever you ask in my name, that I will do because I go to the father. (John 14:13)

In the Old Testament in every instance but one, the word name means character, honor and authority. In the new testament in every instance but one it means character and authority. If we paraphrase this verse you could say it like this... "Whatever you ask the Father for with Christ-like character, He will do it." This is a paraphrase but it is accurate.

Once we understand what the scriptures really mean they unlock mysteries that we can enter into and lay hold of. In the subject of translation by faith, we really can't be guessing about things like this. God gave us the Word and we should be students of the Word.

Study to shew thyself approved unto God, a workman that needeth not to be ashamed, rightly dividing the word of truth. (2 Timothy 2:15)

Why it Matters

When you ask God to use you according to His will and tell Him "your will not mine Lord", you can expect Him to stretch you. If we establish who we are and what God can and will do in us, we can move with the Spirit of God without the baggage of constantly wondering "Is this God?" God established who He is and we need to know it.

Let's list some really pertinent scriptures that challenge the status quo.

I really love ..... Herein is our love made perfect, that we may have boldness in the day of judgment: because as he is, so are we in this world. (1 John 4:17) WOW!

Safe From Deception

Can we really expect the Lord to keep us safe from deception? Is it a promise or just a hope? Are there scriptures? How can we really be sure?

As we seek the Lord and the Kingdom of God we must be vigilant and aware that we do have an enemy that is seeking to devour those that he can. (1 Peter 5:8) The Bible tells us not to be ignorant.

.... Lest Satan should get an advantage of us: for we are not ignorant of his devices.   (2 Corinthians 2:11)

In staying within the safety of the Word, following the Word, we can be safe.

It would be a shame if the more we loved God and closer we wanted to be to Him caused a problem that the Lord could not protect us from the enemy or the enemy's deceptions. Of course He can and does. This is one of the greatest fears that many have concerning "getting too close to God."

The Lord has given us promises and instructions to live by.

Draw nigh to God, and he will draw nigh to you. Cleanse your hands, ye sinners; and purify your hearts, ye double minded. (James 4:8)

But the Lord is faithful. He will establish you and guard you against the evil one. (2Thessalonians 3:3)

I call upon the LORD, who is worthy to be praised, and I am saved from my enemies. (2 Samuel 22:4)

... I will never leave you nor forsake you. (Hebrews 13:5)

There is a Bible full of such wonderful promises. Write down the promises that mean the most to you; the ones that you live by.

Many people believe if they reject all of the supernatural and stay away from learning about or thinking about such spiritual things that this will keep them safe from deception. In a way, I understand the human logic in this. They are believing "if I reject it all, then the "bad" won't be able to influence or harm me." The flaw is, if you reject it all, then you are rejecting the power and presence of God also and in doing this playing right into the enemy's hands. By rejecting all, you really aren't. The enemy's plans are intact and the Lord's supernatural provision is rejected and a person is not safer for having done so. It's like when we were children and we would close our eyes and think that we could not be seen. Don't feel bad though, many of us have been taught this way.

What We Can Do

Whether the Lord has you translocating across the world or teaching a second grade Sunday school class, there are some things that everyone should be doing to stay in that place of safety and confidence in the Lord. Here are a few important things.

The Word

Spending time in the Word is of the utmost importance. We live by the Word and the Word a is a plumb-line by which we can judge the things of our lives. The scripture tells us to "Study to show yourselves approved..... rightly dividing the Word of truth." (2 Timothy 2:15) and that's what we must do.

Spend Time

You'll know the Lord's voice if you spend time with Him. Spend time in prayer and waiting on the Lord and get to know His voice well. Evaluate what your focus is on. Are you focused on the Lord or on doing things for the Lord? Or are you focused on something else entirely?

Keep Short Accounts

Don't let any sin go unconfessed. Repent quickly and don't give the enemy an open door.

Safety in Godly Counsel

Surround yourself with people who have Godly wisdom and bring any concerns you may have to them if you don't feel you have a clear word from God.

Try The Spirits

God would never have told us to do this if we were never going to have to do it. The word says...

Dear friends, do not believe every spirit, but test the spirits to see whether they are from God, because many false prophets have gone out into the world. (1 John 4:1)

For many deceivers have gone out into the world, people who do not confess Jesus as Christ coming in the flesh. This person is the deceiver and the antichrist! (2 John 1:7)

Even seasoned prophets will sometimes put the question to an angel or even the Lord Himself. The Lord nor the angels are offended that you follow this instruction. He gave us this test for a good reason and we must use it.

Bruce's Testimony...

One night as I was in a church teaching, a chariot came into the room. So I asked the Lord "What do I do with that?" because you should dialogue with God and test every spirit. Now there was also a horse there, or a being that looked like a horse so he was the only one I could talk to. So I said "Did Jesus Christ come in the flesh?" and the horse looked at me and said "Yes."

Be Bold and Very Courageous!

God didn't save us to be fearful. All the scriptures that talk about what our relationship with God is supposed to look like are written to bring us into something wonderful and mighty and extraordinary! Look at the lives of the saints and you will see how God wants us to be. We are not shrinking back, but going forward. We are not hiding in fear, but letting our lights shine. We are not yielding to the plans of the enemy, but destroying the works of darkness .

For this purpose the Son of God was manifested, that he might destroy the works of the devil. (1 John 3:8)

As we move into preparations toward translation by faith, be bold, be trusting, know that the Lord never leaves you nor forsakes you and He will guide you in this journey. Believe that He loves you enough that as you seek to commit yourself to Him and His will for your life He will take you to places in God beyond what you have ever imagined.

Fearless Confidence

Many times as we grow up we have experiences, dreams and such that cause us to have some kind of fear in our lives. Sometimes we are taught in church to have fear of supernatural and spiritual things. We may not even remember it but that fear could place a roadblock between us and our calling. When we repent, we break legal rights in the spiritual realm and we can open the pathways for unfettered access.

A Prayer of Repentance

Dear Lord I repent of fear. I repent for any belief that you would not protect me as I seek after you. I repent of fear of the supernatural and spiritual things. You have not given us a spirit of fear Lord so I reject all fear and I turn to you and accept your perfect love and protection. Let a spirit of boldness come upon me. Clothe me with your righteousness because the righteous are bold as a lion. Lord I believe that as I pursue you and the things of your kingdom that you will guide me and lead me into all truth. In Jesus' name, Amen.

Engagement

In this engagement, we are going to build up our spirit so that we can actually begin to start feeling our spirit, knowing we actually are a spirit being and feeling the awareness of that. We already know what the physical reality feels like, we have to learn to shift our awareness to the spiritual.

Have you ever had one of those feeling where the hair on your neck stands up or you feel a strange cold shiver? Many times when manifestations such as these happen it is not a physical thing but rather a physical reaction to a spiritual thing. Your spirit man feels or senses something and for whatever reason your physical body is aware of it and reacts. You will see the reality of this as you engage the angels (or even evil spirits) you will sometimes feel similar feelings and then you become more aware that it actually is a spiritual reality.

We already know how our physical being feels when we pray or worship because that is the realm that we engage in almost exclusively. (The Lord is changing that)

For this engagement, sit still and quietly in your special prayer place where you won't be disturbed and pray quietly in tongues. Being as still and relaxed as you can possibly be, as you pray be consciously aware of how you feel. Because your physical body is not active, your ability to sense your spirit man is increased. The more familiar that feeling is to you, the easier it becomes to move in the spiritual realm. The goal is for it to become natural to walk in both realms just like Adam did or just like Enoch did. After a time start praying in tongues in your imagination or mind. While you do this do not let your mind go blank, you can focus on the words of your prayer (in tongues) or focus on the Lord or a heavenly place. We have all seen pictures of artwork depicting the Lord or Heaven so this shouldn't be hard. All the while though you're trying to stay aware of your spirit.

A variation on this prayer time is praying in tongues silently in your spirit. (imagination) or using the prayer time to decree a powerful verse of scripture such as this verse.

And God raised us up with Christ and seated us with him in the heavenly realms in Christ Jesus. (Ephesians 2:6)

As with most of these engagements, one hour is a starting place. Once you can comfortably do this for an hour you can increase the time spent.

4

INTIMACY WITH GOD

Prepare Yourself

The Lord challenged me on this subject. Is it possible that a man could be translated? I asked the Lord "What is that?" The Lord took me to Acts chapter eight where Philip baptizes the Ethiopian Eunuch and was then instantly twenty seven miles away. The Lord said "That's what I'm talking about." I told Him "Yes Lord. It has to be because you did it." And He said "Good! Prepare yourself!" I said "How do I prepare for that Lord?" He said "By faith."

Well I knew that I did not have to have understanding about this to believe God so I just told the Lord "yes, I believe". Faith. By faith is how we prepare ourselves. All of the processes and exercises and engagements we do, all of the prophetic gestures and prayers and declarations we do it all by faith. That is how we will prepare for translation...by faith.

Walk With God

Genesis 5:24 says ... "And Enoch walked with God..." That's an important key. You have to walk with God. This isn't just a passing acknowledgement that you believe there is a God but a real connection. In the Hebrew when it says that Enoch walked with God, the meaning conveyed is that God was his everything. He was completely sold out. He walked with God. Walking with God is a decision we make. Do you want God to use you?

Then walk with Him. Do you desire that closeness and fellowship? Then walk with Him. This is our choice. Walking in supernatural realities means walking with God.

Learning to Walk With God

As we prepare, we have to realize that this is a process. You may even make a mistake or two along the way but that's ok. We learn to walk with God in much the same way that we would develop any relationship, through fellowship or engagement. There are things that we can do every day to fellowship or engage with God that are simple and powerful. Remember we are doing this by faith! We engage the spiritual realities by faith.

We may start our day by praying "Lord bless us and keep us." But what about after that? Where do we want Jesus in relation to ourselves and our day and our plans? Learn to invite Jesus into every aspect of your life if you truly desire to walk with Him.

"I'm going to work now Lord. Please come with me and stay with me at work." Or "Lord come to the store with me. I always get better bargains when you're there." Maybe invite the Lord for a more intimate fellowship. "Lord lets' you and I go for a walk tonight! Just the two of us!"

Does any of this sound funny or far-fetched? It shouldn't. You see the Lord never leaves us nor forsakes us. These conversations with the Lord are an acknowledgement of this reality and your desire to take advantage of the fact He is with you. If you have ever tasted anything of the unseen realm then you know all too well that this is so true. Those of you who have not yet come to that understanding, you will. Engage in this by faith and it will manifest in greater ways. This causes you to be aware of His presence at all times. This is how you learn to walk with God.

As you seek to Walk With God, what could you do to develop this intimacy?

**Now make a real commitment to do the things on your list to walk closer with God.

A Prayer

Father, Give us greater intimacy with you and teach us to walk with you like Enoch walked with you. Lord be our everything, every day of our lives. As we draw near to you Lord, draw near to us. In Christs' name, Amen

Dying To Self

Dying to self is nothing new to the Christian life. When we are born again, we are alive in Christ and dead to self.

"But you should put aside from you your first way of life, that old man, which is corrupted by deceitful desires..." (Ephesians 4:22)

Therefore if any man is in Christ, he is a new creature; the old things passed away; behold, new things have come. (2 Corinthians 5:17)

Indeed for the successful, normal Christian life we are living in a new reality with new desires and a new purpose. The things that use to be so important no longer are. The things of God are everything now. This is especially true if you desire to live in the deep things of God. Many people occupy the outer courtyard and that's OK but for those whose passion is to remain in the Holy of Holies, there is a dying to self that is born from that passion.

Pursuit is proof of passion! Time spent on God is proof of passion!

If you are really wanting to learn to walk in both realms, to step through the veil and see and go into the spiritual realms then you must die to self. It is a process of continual sanctification. We ask Holy Spirit "Search our hearts Lord and see if there be any wicked way in me." This is a daily consecration to His purposes. Thy will be done Lord. Thy Kingdom come. The biggest problems that people face when seeking this level of relationship is that we have to make a commitment. Only you Lord. No others.

But if serving the LORD seems undesirable to you, then choose for yourselves this day whom you will serve, whether the gods your ancestors served beyond the Euphrates, or the gods of the Amorites, in whose land you are living. But as for me and my household, we will serve the LORD." (Joshua 24:15)

Being Well Pleasing To God

In the scriptures God reveals to us that these who walked in the presence and power of God had testimonies that they pleased God. What pleases God? How do you get it? What qualifies you? Good for us that the scriptures gives us the answer.

By faith Enoch was taken from this life, so that he did not experience death: "He could not be found, because God had taken him away." For before he was taken, he was commended as one who pleased God. (Hebrews 11:5)

Enoch was a cloud walker. He went in the spiritual realms continually. He visited Heaven so much that one day the Lord told him "Enoch, you're here so much, why don't you just stay." Enoch did not taste death, he was translated without having tasted death. One quality that Enoch had that we are certain of is that Enoch sacrificed his own agenda to be with God. To go into the spiritual realm takes time. Time that you have control over. You can choose everyday where you will spend your time, in the physical realm or the spiritual. We can learn to walk in both but it won't drop into your lap. It is a conscious choice that requires something from us.

What pleases God? What could you possibly do? Exercise your faith! Faith pleases God. He has given us so much and we access everything by faith. God loves faith.

But without faith it is impossible to please him: for he that comes to God must believe that he is, and that he is a rewarder of them that diligently seek him. (Hebrews 11:6)

The great thing is that this faith is not something you have to work up or come up with. God has already made the provision. You see all of the things that we need to have an incredible life in Christ, He has provided for us!

For I say, through the grace given unto me, to every man that is among you, not to think of himself more highly than he ought to think; but to think soberly, according as God hath dealt to every man the measure of faith. (Romans 12:3)

As You Go... Remember to encourage others in their journey as well. In faith, speak into their lives and watch God move in your life too.

The Flip-Side of Faith

What is not pleasing to God and how do we stay in that place of being well pleasing to God? God did not make this difficult for us. In any relationship that we really care about, we ask ourselves questions to make sure that the relationship is solid. "Was I too harsh?" "Was I inconsiderate?" "Did I let them know how much they mean to me?" All these questions are especially true if we are talking about love.

The actions and attitudes of the heart that disqualify us from walking in the power of God (such as translation by faith) are the actions of self-centeredness and selfishness. Greed, grumbling, complaining, backbiting, un-thankfulness, and all the evil works of the flesh. The children of Israel wandered in the desert for forty years for this reason. If you keep your heart right, be thankful and seek His will, you will stay in the place of well pleasing. Keep examining your heart. Don't allow yourself to be complacent.

Examine Your Heart.. Is there anything that might be blocking the supernatural things of God from your life? Write them down and pray about it and see what God says.

Guarding Your Heart

To stay in that place of intimacy with God is to stay in a place of unrestricted access and fellowship. A place of walking with Him, day by day and doing what pleases Him. We know from the Word the things that God abhors and we stay far from those things.

Knowing the Word, Knowing Christ

Preparing ourselves for God's plan is a matter of knowing the Word and knowing Christ, the living Word. We know his character because He has revealed it. We know His voice because we listen for it. The Bible says...

My sheep hear my voice, and I know them, and they follow me: (John 10:27)

This is a very declarative statement. Jesus said we hear his voice. Going into the spiritual realms this is very important. It may sound funny to say but if you are in the spirit and have an encounter you want to know how to handle it or if you don't , be able to hear God's voice clearly so as to deal with whatever the situation is. There is not time to run and get your Bible and figure it out in the moment.

Know the Word. Study the Word. Know Christ and develop an ever closer relationship with Him. Would you like a good starting place? If you are wondering about recognizing God's voice, start with the things that Jesus has said that are recorded in the New Testament. Study these scriptures and meditate on them. What is the heart of Jesus concerning the lost, the dying, the hurting, the religious or the faithful? All these things are revealed in the "words in red."

Getting to Know You

What are some of the things that you would love to know about the Lord? It doesn't have to be some deep theological thing, just something you may have wondered about. Such as ...Does the Lord have a sense of humor? Or does He have favorite colors? Or even what are some of the things He enjoys doing.

Now, make a list of three questions that you would ask Him if you had the chance.

*Try to choose questions that mean something to you.

Read The Beatitudes (John 5-7)

What can you tell us about Jesus after reading this passage? Describe Him and tell us about his character. What is important to Him? What do you know about Him?

Established

Ok... This is basic Christianity you say. Yes it is. This thing about knowing Christ and knowing his character and knowing his attributes is about knowing and moving from a place of faith and strength into the spiritual realms. The Lord will not throw you into a situation that you are not willing to be prepared for. He loves you too much. To go into these heavenly places you have to be grounded. Grounded in the word and grounded in your relationship. That's why "little" things like this are so important.

Mike's Testimony...

It was the middle of 2014 when my sister called me to come help her as her car had quit running. She couldn't get it started so I went to see if I could help. While we were standing there at her car with the hood up, a man who has helped me and kind of watched over me during my life showed up and asked if I needed his help. I said "No, we'll be ok." He then walked up to the car, looked under the hood and then looked at me. "You have to be well grounded because of the power involved." He said that a couple of times. I thanked him and he left. That man who stopped to help that day and has been watching over me during my life was Philip.... the same Philip who baptized the Ethiopian Eunuch. He made a special trip to specifically tell me it is important to be grounded. If Heaven takes it seriously, we must also.

The preparation is the establishment of the relationship, knowing who you are in Christ, knowing your legal rights and authority and knowing your mandate. What has God called you to do? That is what He has prepared you for.

Engagement

It's one thing to go through the scriptures and learn about Christ, his nature and character but it's another thing entirely to ask him face to face.

Go into a time of quiet prayer, such as has already been described and in your imagination go into one of the Bible stories and see Jesus and ask him face to face the three questions that you have written out. Remember to exercise all of your spiritual senses as you engage by faith the Lord Jesus. See your surroundings, feel the atmosphere and temperature. Is it calm or windy? What are the smells you smell? Create in your imagination the entire scene. Remember, this is a doorway, a portal into the spiritual realm. If you can lay hold of this by faith, you can have it.

A Prayer

Father, As we seek to follow you and walk in your ways, Give us grace and strength to learn stillness before you. Teach us to be still and know that you are God. As you teach us to access these ancient pathways and doorways and portals, activate us to enter in and teach us by giving us spectacular experiences to show us how real this is and also give us peace and assurance by your Holy Spirit. In Jesus' name, Amen

Engagement

Speaking God's word over yourself or others is an incredible way to see or feel the reality of the spiritual realm. This is especially true when you declare who you are in Christ or declare your position of authority in Christ.

As we are still learning to discern our spirits, or our spiritual being and differentiate between our body, soul and spirit, this is another excellent exercise to cause you to feel your spirit as you react spiritually to the Word of God being spoken over you. (As you speak it over yourself)

Write down a verse or a declaration based on a verse to use as you speak the Word over yourself.. Then record any feelings, sensations, sights or sounds you experience. Be as specific as possible

...As He is, so are we in this world... (1John 4:17)

5

COMMITMENT

In preparing to journey into the spiritual realms or operate in the power of God for any reason, there is a price. No it isn't money. You pay with your life...

For which of you, desiring to build a tower, doth not first sit down and count the cost, whether he have wherewith to complete it? (Luke 14:28)

In section one, we talked about whether we had legal rights and precedent in the Word to access the Heavenly realm. In this chapter we will examine commitment and yielding to the Lord's plans and purposes in accessing the Heavenly realm.

I know that most of you would not even be reading or studying this topic if you were not already aware of the cost involved. It is important to talk about these things though because if you feel you are doing everything right and are still not breaking through in the spirit, you can make assessments if you have all the info.

Everyone Has The Same 24 Hours ...More or Less

It is an ongoing misconception that it is easier for some people to press in than others. "Brother I have a family!" "Really? Me too." "Well I have to work every day!" "Wow, what a coincidence." "Well I shouldn't have to give up my free time!"

Now we are getting to the bottom of this. You see all of us have responsibilities and obligations. We all have bills to pay and places that we have to be. It is not always easy or convenient to live this lifestyle of walking in both realms. These are things we have to consider. We seriously have to make this a priority in our lives. I'm not talking about sacrificing our responsibilities as parents or not providing for our loved ones or being irresponsible. Many people claim to live by faith but are really just living irresponsibly and expecting God (or their relatives) to bail them out every week from their own poor choices.

No, by God's own Word we are responsible to take care of our families and responsibilities. We are talking about something else.

But if any provide not for his own, and especially for those of his own house, he has denied the faith, and is worse than an unbeliever. (1 Timothy 5:8)

Spending Time In Heaven

After hearing a spectacular testimony once from someone whom the Lord had taken to Heaven for six hours, I heard a friend say "I'd love to spend six hours in Heaven!" And to be fair, I know he would. Who wouldn't right? The problem is that you would have to commit six hours of your time to do it. I knew this man, and as much as I love him he does not have the desire to wait on the Lord for an hour, let alone six hours. This is the crux of the problem for many people. I suggested to someone once, "Give up your Saturday" because I knew he had no obligations on Saturday. He got angry and said "My Saturdays belong to me!"

Everyone I know that has unfettered or even remotely unfettered access to the spiritual realm has placed their time in the Lord's hands. Not one of them would say "Lord, I really wanted to just spend the day watching reruns on TV. But I'll be available for you tomorrow."

This is not to say that the Lord puts undue demands on you or tries to "ruin" your life. All the things you enjoy, (or most of them) God created so that you could have pleasure. Going out to eat with the family or shooting baskets with your kids etc., are things the Lord knows we enjoy and He is not trying to strip these things from us. He is only trying to strip the priority of these things from being above Him. Jesus came to give us life!

The thief comes not, but to steal, and to kill, and to destroy: I am come that they might have life, and that they might have it more abundantly. (John 10:10)

To those who have experienced God at this level there is no issue here.

What are your priorities? List the top five in order of importance.

Now examine your list. Is there anything that would conflict with being on God's schedule? Is there any event that would cause you to tell the Lord I'm sorry but I can't miss this? Is there any activity that comes close in importance to you? No? Good! If we seek first the Kingdom of God, all these other things will be added to us!

So now we know it will take a commitment of time from us. How much time exactly? That depends on how much you desire to reach your destination. At first you will very likely need to spend focused time away from the natural or physical realm to even learn to move in the spiritual realm. The laying down of the physical accelerates the spiritual process. It will vary person to person. Some people may have to spend hours a day for weeks or months and some will not.

Passion is a Key

If you have an intense passion and desire for the Lord and the things of the Lord this will also speed things up for you. The thing to remember here is that it is natural for you to move easily in the natural realm. You can walk, talk, run, eat, smell, discern physical things and judge things all because you have spent 20 or 30 or 40 years (or however old you are) continually engaged with the physical realm. The process is similar with the spiritual. The more time you can spend in the spiritual realm the faster you will acclimate to it. Time spent in pursuit is proof of passion.

A Shift Will Happen

After a while, it's different for everyone, you will find that you can stay engaged with the spiritual realm even while fully engaged in the physical. You will be able to maintain that awareness all the time. You can do this because you actively pursue it. Continually practicing the presence of God will make this a reality in your life. The more you stay aware, the more it will manifest and the clearer and stronger it will become. Some will walk in both realms at the same time and some will move back and forth.

The Death of Pride

When you are talking about the supernatural things of God, the death of pride is a real issue on a couple of different levels. The group of people in the church world who believe that God did supernatural things in the past, or that the Bible is a real and accurate truth, has become less and less through the recent past. Sin has crept in and manifested to the point that many denominations are making up their own "truth" as if it doesn't matter. The group of people who believe God did miracles in the past and still does is much , much less. The people who believe that everything in the Bible is true and accurate and also believe that we can live in this reality now, are just a handful of those who claim the name "Christian."

What does this mean? This means that we are the "fringe" according to the religious system and the world. Those who believe in healing are looked at kind of sideways but those that talk with the Lord face to face or with angels and saints are considered delusional. (According to a friend who is a physician) Take that up a notch when you talk about moving supernaturally across the heavens or the world. There is no room for pride here. Most of the world and a lot of the church distain the supernatural things of God therefore they won't think very highly of you either.

Remember what I told you: 'A servant is not greater than his master.' If they persecuted me, they will persecute you also. If they obeyed my teaching, they will obey yours also. (John 15:20)

I have seen people mock those who said they believed that the gold dust phenomenon is real and them mock them when they saw it manifest in front of them. It doesn't matter what proof you give, many do not want to believe because they would have to examine their lives in the light of the fact that God truly does exist. They don't want to do that.

Also, God hates pride. Pride is rebellion and it is as the sin of witchcraft and is a major blockage to receiving the power and presence of God if it exists within us. Pride will keep you from seeing and going into the spiritual realm.

But he gives more grace. Therefore it says, "God opposes the proud, but gives grace to the humble." (James 4:6)

Humility, a Major Key

When the Lord began to teach me about this subject, He led me to Isaiah chapter six.

In the year that King Uzziah died, I saw the Lord sitting on a throne, high and lifted up, and the train of His robe filled the temple. 2 Above it stood seraphim; each one had six wings: with two he covered his face, with two he covered his feet, and with two he flew. 3 And one cried to another and said:

"Holy, holy, holy is the Lord of hosts; The whole earth is full of His glory!" 4 And the posts of the door were shaken by the voice of him who cried out, and the house was filled with smoke. 5 So I said: "Woe is me, for I am undone! Because I am a man of unclean lips, And I dwell in the midst of a people of unclean lips; For my eyes have seen the King, The Lord of hosts."

6 Then one of the seraphim flew to me, having in his hand a live coal which he had taken with the tongs from the altar. 7 And he touched my mouth with it, and said: "Behold, this has touched your lips; Your iniquity is taken away, And your sin purged." 8 Also I heard the voice of the Lord, saying: "Whom shall I send, And who will go for Us?"

Then I said, "Here am I! Send me." 9 And He said, "Go, and tell this people: 'Keep on hearing, but do not understand; Keep on seeing, but do not perceive.' (Isaiah 6:1-9)

Why is it that Isaiah, a Prophet well educated and renowned throughout all of Israel, did not have a vision of God until King Uzziah died? What was it about King Uzziah's death that triggered a vision of God?

As I studied this, I found in second Chronicles chapter twenty-six it says this...

But when he was strong his heart was lifted up, to his destruction, for he transgressed against the Lord his God by entering the temple of the Lord to burn incense on the altar of incense. (2 Chronicles 26:16)

That is the key. From the age of sixteen he followed God all his life but somewhere in his latter years pride came in. It caused him to die. The Lord gave me this revelation...Isaiah chapter six could be read this way... "In the year that pride died, I saw the Lord."

The Lord did a deeper work in Isaiah that led him to this greater dimension, and he saw the Lord, high and lifted up.

Maintaining Our Relationship With God

In preparation for going and moving in the spiritual realm, it is important that we are close to the Lord. We have to know His voice. We have to know His ways. We should keep ourselves pure before Him so that the enemy has no open door to us and we stay safe from deceptions.

In the spiritual realm, things can be a little challenging at times. Being as we have not lived this life of walking in both realms for too long (at least for most of us) it is an adjustment and a learning process. We maintain our relationship so that the potential for deception is minimized. Any sin we try to hold onto going into these realms becomes an open door to give the enemy access to influence us or deceive us in some way.

You will be constantly learning by the Holy Spirit what is normal. How to move and how to act. How we should behave and how we should communicate. Where we should and shouldn't go etc.. You will encounter beings that navigate these realms and you will interact with them. Some of them are of the Lord. You already read the testimony of challenging the horse with "Did Jesus come in the flesh?" You will be constantly learning as you go. Don't be in fear, just be wise. Be diligent. There are angels watching over you and they will keep you safe and help you to acclimate to this realm. They will instruct you and even rebuke you if needed. Learn to appreciate and honor the angels around your life. We are not talking about worshipping angels as so many people are apparently afraid that they might do. You won't worship them...They wouldn't let you. We honor them in the same way that you would honor anyone else in ministry, as a co-laborer.

I, John, am the one who heard and saw these things. And when I had heard and seen them, I fell down to worship at the feet of the angel who had been showing them to me. But he said to me, "Don't do that! I am a fellow servant with you and with your fellow prophets and with all who keep the words of this scroll. Worship God!" (Revelation 22:8-9)

A Prayer

Father, help me to be diligent in my pursuit of you and the things of the Kingdom. Fill me fresh everyday with your spirit and let the desires of my heart be born of you. Give me a burning passion for you and set a hedge around me so that nothing can steal away my attention toward you. Father let my commitment to you be steadfast and established in heavenly places. As you use me in miraculous ways help me to stay humble before you. In Jesus' name, Amen.

Engagement

Pick a time that you can commit to every day for prayer and waiting on the Lord. Engage the Lord at that time every day for a week. Wait on God or pray or worship, mainly focusing on how you feel about that time with the Lord. Is it a time that you feel you are making a connection? Is it easy to feel His presence at this time? Are you able to stay awake? (For those choosing a night-watch) Write down your experiences and feelings, sensations and also the practical, physical side of choosing this time. Then repeat the process using other chosen times. It may take a little time but you will find that "sweet" time that everything just seems to flow so beautifully and you'll know what works best for you.

*You may very well have to do this many times before you discover your favorite time.

6

ADJUSTING TO THE SPIRITUAL DIMENSION

The spiritual dimension is one that always requires adjusting to. Specifically knowing when we enter it is a learning process. Going into this dimension or the realization that you are going into this dimension usually begins to happen to most people at night when they're asleep or close to sleep or waking from sleep. This is why many people relegate spiritual experiences to dream status. Starting out, as you experience spiritual things you may believe that you are only dreaming.

The thing to be very aware of however is that you don't want to allow yourself to believe that. "Oh, it was just a dream." Allowing yourself to believe that these experiences are dreams, dismisses them. Especially if you know that God is raising you up and training you for this thing called Translation by Faith.

As you experience your first journeys in the spirit or in the physical dimension, (translation / translocation) always take care to acknowledge that these are real journeys and training exercises that the Lord is taking you through.

Journal all of your experiences as reality and look at them as reality and if you do this, you will increase in awareness in the experience and about the experience. You give yourself permission to accept this as normal and as you continually move into this realm even the shift from one dimension to another increases in conscious awareness.

The Atmosphere of the Spirit Realm

When you enter the spirit realm, one thing you will probably notice right away is that everything including the atmosphere is alive. The "air" around you will seem to be vibrating or living in some way. Your senses will be heightened so much that it will almost be like you were previously dead or asleep and suddenly now you are awake. You will have the ability to know and communicate with objects, things that are hard to classify, the weather, angels or evil spirits without ever saying a word. You operate at a totally superior level that must be experienced to be believed or understood.

The Natural Realm Pales In Comparison To The Spiritual Realm

Something to keep in mind for future exercises and the engagement of the spiritual realm is the descriptions just made as well as descriptions of others who have experienced these realms. As you wait on God and engage in your imagination the spiritual realm, you can "look" for these things or sensations that have been described. It's kind of like if someone sent you somewhere in the natural and described the places you were going to see. You would then know you had arrived.

Beings in the Spiritual Realm

In the spirit there are many things, many beings besides angels and evil spirits. The are many classes of angels and they can dress or appear different from each other. Some wear tunic type outfits and some wear "normal" clothing that we might see today. Some angels are dressed in battle armor and some are clothed in light or fire.

Mike's Testimony...

The angel that I see most often appears as fire or a bright light that looks like fire. He is almost always standing to my left and manifests his presence a lot, especially when I pray or think about heavenly things.

Sometimes you might see beings that in your natural reasoning you could assume are not good, but in reality they are. If you look at the descriptions in Ezekiel or in

Revelation you can see how appearances can be deceiving if you take things on face value. That is why it's so important to be filled with the Spirit and to be Spirit led.

There are objects of all types, shapes and things that are hard to classify that have personalities. You can communicate with them. Some good, some bad. We have to discern good from evil and that's where exercising our senses comes into play.

You might think that these types of things would be scary. In fact some people have told me "Pray that I stop seeing in the spirit because sometimes I see demons and I don't like that." I tell them that that's a good thing! If you can see an evil spirit then it can't sneak up on you! If you can see them you can rebuke them and make them go away.

The Physical Side

When some people are drawn into the spirit it doesn't even feel like it is odd. They can experience fully both realms and act independently in both realms at the same time.

Bruce's Testimony...

I was preaching at a church in Coeur D'Alene Idaho and had felt that God was going to do something spectacular that night so I asked a photographer friend to come and take pictures as the Spirit led. I had thought that perhaps there might be manifestation of the angels or something. I really wasn't certain.

As I spoke, I was suddenly caught up out of my body and ascended into the stars, far above the Earth. I could see Eastern Europe from that position and the outline of a country. I asked the Lord, "Lord is that Lithuania or Latvia?" He said "Latvia."

I then descended towards the country and found myself above a little town I was lowered straight through the roof of an apartment building and into a hallway, standing in front of apartment two-twelve. I entered the apartment and found a little girl crying in a room. I spoke to her and ministered to her and prayed with her concerning problems in their family. Then I came back to Coeur D'Alene. All the while having continued preaching.

I had forgotten all about the photos my friend was taking and remembered six months later and called him. "Whatever happened to those photos?" I asked him. He said "Well...That's a problem. You see when you were speaking I took a picture of you and in the picture you are completely transparent. I've had experts look at the film and examine it and it was determined that this was impossible."

The Lord had done something miraculous that night and even gave a supernatural sign and wonder to verify the event.

Sometimes God will take you to two or even three places at the same time.

"I am the LORD, the God of all mankind. Is anything too hard for me? (Jeremiah 32:27)

Sometimes people are drawn into the spirit and they get physically very tired or feel very heavy. They are aware that they are going places in the spirit but have limited ability to interact in the physical realm during that time. Many times when this happens the spiritual aspect overwhelms them and they shake or vibrate intensely without much control or can also become drunk in the spirit.

Sometimes this happens for extended periods of time especially when the Lord launches people into ministry. A time of preparation.

The ability to operate in the natural and operate in the spiritual realm at the same time seems to be born out of a lifestyle of continually engaging the spiritual realm. Regardless of what you are doing, if you make room for this reality it will allow you to walk in both realms at the same time.

Can you think of any verses that verify that we can be in two places at once?

Have you ever experienced the Spirit of God in power this way? Recall the experience and write down what you can remember of it.

We will be re-visiting this soon!

Working With Angels

One thing we can be very glad about is that we do not travel these realms alone. We have the promise of the Lord...

Let your manners be without covetousness, contented with such things as you have; for he hath said: I will not leave thee, neither will I forsake thee. (Hebrews 13:5)

We also know that He has given His angels charge over us. As you move through the spiritual realm you come to an understanding that angels are not mindless robots that have to be told everything. They are quite powerful and quite intelligent. They can see problems forming before we do and are at work to set things straight before we ever realize it. We have to make sure that we always speak in faith what the Word says so as not to prevent them or hinder them in any way. They also have personalities and can interact with us. Sometimes angels are very serious and they have serious business and other times they are quite light-hearted and joyful. Angels can have a sense of humor and angels can also be offended by our behavior. Angels can appear to be happy or sad or even angry. Some very serious angels even look kind of angry.

Angels Will Partner With You

Angels are ministering spirits sent forth to minister on behalf of the heirs of salvation. (That's us) The work that God has called us to do is impossible in the natural. His angels play a huge role in everything going on in our lives. As you learn and adjust to moving in the realm of the kingdom, prepare to be seeing them and working with them a lot.

Bless The Angels

Start "watering the soil" of your relationships with the angels. How? By prayer. Pray for the angels around your life, family, ministry and church. Bless them and decree empowerment to them. You don't have to get weird with it, just ask for God's will to be done in their lives. That's safe.

Bless the LORD, O my soul: and all that is within me, bless his holy name. (Psalm 103:1)

The big problem that most people who were raised in the church have with angels is due to a slightly skewed view that has been presented about angels. There has been this idea prevalent in the church that we are not supposed to acknowledge or interact with the angels in any way. If we do acknowledge them it constitutes worship. This idea is totally un-biblical. You don't have to know much about the scriptures to know that all throughout the Bible there are encounters with angels. There are people talking to angels, getting direction from angels, getting rebuked by angels and even making them meals. Interaction with angels is normal for believers! Or at least it's supposed to be. We have to start cultivating our relationship with the angels afresh. Like any relationship or friendship it takes some effort and some desire on our part.

Honest conversation

Even if you don't have fellowship with angels, you have to be comfortable enough that you can listen to them and let them help you. If every time an angel shows up to help you, you rebuke him in Jesus' name, that's not a good scenario. We have to discern. We have to exercise our senses to discern. When you talk to them or with them let it be with a level of respect for who they are both to you and to the Lord. They are important. You can be close to someone and still respect them. We're not talking about being overly familiar.

Think about this... if you were helping someone, looking after them and blessing them every day but they never acknowledged you or your efforts on their behalf how would you feel about them. You say you have relationships like that? I think we all do. Don't make that mistake with them. Angels are an integral part of ministry regardless of what the size and scope of your ministry is. Be mindful of that fact.

Just like we stay aware that the Lord is always with us, we should also be aware that angels are too. Tell the Lord that you are grateful for the presence of the angels

A Prayer

Father, Thank you for giving your angels charge over us. Thank you that they protect us night and day. Thank you for the angels who minister to us and with us for the Kingdom. Father bless the angels around our lives and empower them with greater measures of your power for their purpose. Bless them with every good blessing that you have set aside for the angels. Father set a guard over my tongue so that I don't speak in unbelief or anything that would hinder their efforts on our behalf. In Jesus' name. Amen.

Engaging the Kingdom

For this engagement we are going to take the experience that we wrote about and re-enter it. This as with everything we access is done by faith. The more you access this realm by faith the clearer it becomes.

So take a position that you feel most comfortable in to do this. Relax and ask the Lord to help you. Such as "Father, I desire to revisit that time that you ......" Now think about that moment and relive as much of it as you possibly can. Relive the moments before it even began and then continue into the experience. Of course once again feel the sensations, the emotions, the atmosphere and really "lean" into it.

Keep focusing on it while in a relaxed manner. Pay attention to how you feel physically and notice whether you feel an awareness that is separate from your physical self.

This is totally opposite from doing something in the physical realm. Moving into the spiritual realm is not so much a matter of doing but of being aware and taking steps of faith.

Journal The Experience

7

SPIRITUAL DOORWAYS AND ACCESS

Spiritual doorways are access points or places that exist or that you create through faith. Just like a doorway in the natural allows you access to a physical place, a spiritual doorway provides access to spiritual places. In the physical world you can see or feel a door or a doorway. You can feel a wind or breeze sometimes when you open a door in the natural. A shift of environment is normal when you go through a doorway. You are moving from one place to another...from outside to inside, from inside to outside, from heat to air conditioning etc.. Changes happen even in the natural when we go through doorways.

In the spirit realm it is the same. When we go through spiritual doorways we also move from one place to another, from one environment to another. The doorways or gateways or access points will not seem very tangible when you first begin to engage them. This is very much a walk of faith especially at first before you experience the manifestation of what these doorways bring.

We are going to explain some of these doorways and tell you how we access them and what the whole process looks like. Understanding increases the more we practice.

The fact that other religions take Biblical principles and twist them to their own purpose has no bearing on whether or not we should follow the scriptures those principles are drawn from. We keep them all. We follow them all.

When we are talking about accessing the ancient pathways or doorways into the things of the spirit we are really talking about developing a discipline. We have to make ourselves available to the Lord. It's not always easy when we begin this journey because we normally have little or no manifestation in the beginning of the reality of it, so it can seem like a colossal waste of time. This is also true about developing our spiritual senses or even in beginning to lay hold of the gifts of the spirit.

The things we have to do to engage translation by faith sometimes takes time to develop. There are many factors involved and there is no "one size fits all" formula. Everyone is different with different obstacles and issues. One practical way to look at this is as if you are going to the gym to get in shape. You can go to the gym your first day and work really hard for two, three or even four hours. But when you look in the mirror at the end of the workout you won't see any visible changes. You could throw in the towel and say "This exercise stuff doesn't work" but the truth is that it is a process. You may be in a position to experience amazing things your first day or it may take a few days, weeks or even months. But remember that God is doing a quick work in these present days.

Another big mistake that some make is by reverting back to that old prayer model of continuing to ask God for hour after hour to sovereignly give us the thing we desire. He has already given it. We just need to follow the example of those who have gone before us, the forerunners. We have to lay hold of these doors by faith and engage until we have an awareness of the manifestation of them.

Another thing we have to understand is that our spirits already live in the spirit realm. We already experience things in the spirit but because there is a lack of integration or participation between our body. soul and spirit, we lack a conscious awareness of the activities of our spirit.

Mike's Testimony...

There is an angel that takes me places. For the most part he has taken me places to introduce me to other angels who are or will be working with us or to garner provision for our ministry. One day we went to what looked like a casual office type environment and I was going to be introduced to someone who was to help me with computer stuff.

When we arrived, there was another angel that was also there that was happy to see me and he came and started talking to me like we were old friends and I didn't have a clue as to who he was. He kept saying "It's me!" and then he would state his name. He was surprised that I didn't know him and then he said his name again and when I still didn't get it, he said "Doren! You know, Doren!" When he said Doren, it was as if a light came on and I knew exactly who he was. He was a good friend. Later I felt kind of embarrassed that I didn't recognize him. When I came back from that realm, I went online and looked up the name Doren. It's a Hebrew name that means "Gift". It was then that I really realized that we experience things that we aren't always consciously aware of or don't always remember.

To reiterate something... If you want to live and walk in both realms, you have to live and walk in both realms.

Most people have experiences where they feel like they have gone somewhere or have been somewhere before and there is a vague recollection of the event. This could very well be actual memories of events and not of dreams.

Think about your own experiences and see if there is one that stands out to you. If there is, write it down with the key points or as much of it as you can remember.

This memory and really any memory of some experience that you have had in the spirit realm is a powerful doorway to enter in again. Once you have been somewhere it is much easier to access that place again. Engage that memory and go back into it. See what happens and write down your degree of success in doing so.

The Power of Stillness

"Be still, and know that I am God. I will be exalted among the nations, I will be exalted in the earth!" (Psalms 46:10)

The word used here, râphâh , means properly to cast down; to let fall; to let hang down; and to be relaxed, especially the hands: Not making an effort or exerting oneself.

Tremble, and do not sin; Meditate in your heart upon your bed, and be still. Selah. (Psalms 4:4)

Stillness is a place where you have felt the distinction between spirit and flesh. In your prayer time or worship or waiting on the Lord time, being still is something you should practice according to the scriptures. When you take the definitions above and apply them to your prayer time, how would you do it? How would you describe it?

Stillness, especially the physical part can be learned and practiced. The easiest way to do this is by praying or meditating while in a relaxed position such as lying down (as in Psalms 4:4) or by sitting in a comfortable chair or recliner. Then as you pray, every few minutes do a physical check. Are you relaxed? Is every part of you relaxed? How about your hands? (Psalms 46) Are they relaxed or have they tensed up? For most people, even when you are consciously trying to stay relaxed and still, there is still a tendency for certain support muscles to try to tighten or flex. If you continually check yourself, you can relax again and continue. Through repeated practice you can learn to stay pretty still and then your awareness of your spirit man becomes much greater. You see any focus at all on the physical distracts our ability to become aware of our spirit. This is especially true when you are first learning. After you have gained this awareness you can interact with people, walk, talk and minister while still engaging the spiritual realm or the spiritual part of your being.

That is how some ministers can actually be ministering in two or three places at the same time. There is that "walking" in the supernatural realm from spending so much time there. Just like Enoch!

Waiting on God

This is putting yourself in a place for God to show you something or tell you something by waiting for Him or with Him. There is something about waiting on God that the Lord honors when we do it. We are making a statement. "Your presence is more important than anything else I could be doing."

Lead me in Your truth and teach me, For You are the God of my salvation; For You I wait all the day. (Psalms 25:5)

We come to an understanding that we have to have God speak to us or show us something because apart from Him we can do nothing. What did Jesus say?

Jesus gave them this answer: "Very truly I tell you, the Son can do nothing by himself; he can do only what he sees his Father doing, because whatever the Father does the Son also does. (John 5:19)

Waiting on the Lord is one of the premier things that you can do to position yourself for walking in the supernatural. Can we really wait on the Lord "all the day" like David did? If you examine the lives of those in the recent history of the church who moved in great power, you will always find that they spent incredible amounts of time alone with God.

The Night Watch

If you wait on the Lord in the watch of the night you will find an even greater time of access to the spiritual realm. One of the reasons is that there are very few things to distract us or engage our physical senses. No one is moving around at three am. There's not enough light to really see anything, no phone calls and no barriers. In the night watch the brightness of heavenly things stand out against the dark. These are things we can notice and appreciate as the Lord shows us.

** The things we are talking about are not mutually exclusive. We can apply all or some depending on the leading of the Holy Spirit. Put stillness, waiting on the Lord and the night watch all together and see what happens!

Meditation

Let the words of my mouth and the meditation of my heart be acceptable in your sight, O LORD, my rock and my Redeemer. (Psalms 19:14)

Let my meditation be pleasing to Him; As for me, I shall be glad in the LORD.   (Psalms 104:34)

Meditation according to the dictionary is the act of thinking quietly. While the carnal man may meditate with his mind, the sons of God meditate in their hearts. The carnal mind is enmity against God. What we carry in our hearts is born of God and therefore we meditate in our hearts those things that are pleasing to Him. Meditate on the Word of God. Meditate on His goodness and His attributes. Meditate on His blessings and His presence. Be aware and acknowledge His presence and invite His presence to become greater still. As you meditate, be aware .

Meditation on the Word or the things of God is yet another way that we engage and develop our spirit man to be able to function normally as we were created to function.

One very practical thing you can do is to take a scripture verse and read it through. Then read the verse again more slowly, pause and think about the verse then read it again. Now re-read the verse again but this time put the stress on different words or highlight different words as you go through it. Think about those words within the verse and what they mean and the impact that they can have on you. Ask the Holy Spirit to give you greater revelation each time you read through it.

Choose a verse to practice this meditation on scripture. Go through the verse as outlined above and write any observations or new revelations.

The Sanctified Imagination

In the Word Jesus gives us a powerful key that can literally transform our lives. The key is found in Matthew chapter five.

But I say to you that whoever looks at a woman to desire her has already committed adultery with her in his heart. (Mathew 5:28)

Jesus is saying very clearly that He considers imagination as reality. If we can take hold of this reality we can make great strides in seeing and entering in the spirit. This is also a major place of opposition from the enemy and we need to be aware of that. It's not a problem that ungodly thoughts come. The problem is that we cannot engage and meditate on those thoughts. Any thought that is not lovely or pure we dismiss right away and move our thoughts back to the things of God.

Jesus said unto him, Thou shalt love the Lord thy God with all thy heart, and with all thy soul, and with all thy mind. (Matthew 22:37)

In this scripture the word mind is actually the Greek work dianoia. The word dianoia means imagination.

Jesus is saying love the Lord your God with your imagination! How do we do that? It's the same thing we do when we love someone. We think about the person, maybe see what they might be doing right now, think about how they look or smell or the sound of their laughter. All this is done in the imagination and that's what we do with God.

We have already mentioned this to some degree but this is an important area that is a launching place for moving into the spirit. We have to understand this. In almost everything that we do in the Kingdom we engage our imaginations. Our imagination is a creative force. God created all things by first seeing them or imagining them.

The more we allow ungodly or unclean thoughts to permeate our imaginations, the more the enemy will put up blockages or veils to make it hard for us to look on the unseen. Keep your mind fixed on Him.

Our ability to move and see in the unseen realm is greatly enhanced as we exercise our senses and exercise our imaginations.

Try This Exercise

Make yourself still and quiet and pick a place in your mind / imagination. Now go to that place (in your imagination) and begin to "see" the surroundings. Also look at the weather, the family , smell the smells and sense the atmosphere. Your ability to do this as realistically as possible is the degree to which you will be able to engage the spiritual realm.

Establishing a Doorway

This next exercise for the imagination is specifically done to develop a doorway for moving in the spiritual realm.

First, find a doorway that you walk through a lot, possibly in your home or some other familiar place. Examine this doorway. Look at the shape and style of the door casings, the color. The texture and any other characteristics that you can notice. Study it. Step through it and remember the sights associated with stepping through. When you first do this, to really get familiar you may have to step through in the natural and then close your eyes and step through in your imagination. Do this over and over until it becomes easy to see the doorway as you step through in your imagination. Now add another part. Now as you step through, make a declaration as you do. "I am stepping through this doorway from the natural to the spiritual realm." Or "From the natural to the supernatural." Next, when you do this in your imagination also declare in your imagination the same thing.

Now in your imagination, as you step through the doorway, "see" a difference on the other side of that doorway. When you step through, see the air as alive and colorful. "See" angels in the distance or close by. This is a kind of prophetic act or prophetic gesture kind of like when Moses spoke to the rock to activate the water to come out.

The clearer and more real we can make this doorway, the easier it will be to go through it into the spiritual realm.

Do this every day for a week and record any progress, what it feels like. Whether or not you begin to feel the spiritual realm when you step through etc..

Being a Worshipper

You are holy, enthroned on the praises of Israel. (Psalms 22:3)

Being a worshipper is to bring the atmosphere of Heaven around you, or to bring yourself into the Heavenly places. Angels love to be around worshippers and that atmosphere. Worship carries with it the attitude of thanksgiving, of appreciation. An acknowledgement of what He has done for us. We see our desperate need for Him and how He fulfills that need and it causes that attitude of worship.

Worship aloud and worship in the spirit and worship in both places simultaneously.

If we look at the meaning of the word worship it denotes a physical posture of being knelt down prone before God. It isn't always possible to take this position in the natural but we can in the spirit / imagination at any time at all.

We will come back to worship in an upcoming section.

Prophetic Gestures and Activations

In the bible, we see the prophets doing things that are directed by the spirit of God. Things like Moses speaking to the rock to give water, Aaron throwing down the staff to become a snake and Elisha throwing the stick in the water to make the axe head float in 2 Kings 6:6.

These gestures are acts or steps of faith, kind of like the stepping through the doorway we talked about earlier. These actions taken in faith and directed by the Spirit have tremendous power.

Two Gestures / Activations

Here are two prophetic gestures specifically for the subjects we're studying.

1. Pulling Down Veils

This first gesture is great for those whose spiritual vision is not yet clear. (That would be most of the church so don't feel bad)

Out loud, declare "In Jesus' name I pull down the veils and scales from my eyes."

When you do this, make the physical movement of pulling down the veils just like you would if they were physically covering your eyes.

2. Stepping Through

This gesture is also a very simple act of faith.

Simply take one step forward and declare "Father, I am stepping into the realm of your Kingdom.' Now, take a step back and declare " Father, I am now stepping back into the natural realm."

We do it both ways because we move back and forth from the natural to the spiritual and visa-versa.

Think about your own walk and circumstances. **Create a prophetic gesture** that would help your life and spiritual goals. Write out the physical and verbal part and what it should help accomplish.

Declarations and Decrees

A decree is an official order issued by a legal authority. As heirs of God and joint heirs with Jesus Christ, we are legal heirs of the Kingdom of our father. We are given authority to speak things to see them come to pass in God's word.

Thou shalt also decree a thing, and it shall be established unto thee: and the light shall shine upon thy ways. (Job 22:28)

Death and life are in the power of the tongue, and those who love it will eat its fruits. (Proverbs 18:21)

Truly I tell you, whatever you bind on earth will be bound in heaven, and whatever you loose on earth will be loosed in heaven. (Matthew 18:18)

On the authority of the word of God create several decrees fitting your journey into translation by faith and the supernatural realms.

Spiritual Sight as a Door

It is much easier to move into the spiritual realm if you can see it. Maybe because you aren't going completely by faith but also having the solidness of the manifestation of that realm. Spiritual sight is an incredible access point for moving into the supernatural. There are many things that we can do to develop this and the exercises in this workbook will also be of tremendous benefit to increase spiritual sight.

An overview of things we would engage to open our spiritual eyes would be things like awareness, imagination, actively looking, repentance, forgiveness, asking, praying, fasting, meditating, interceding, blessing, receiving impartations, atmospheres, worshipping and other things. This is also a subject that if you truly desire to see the unseen there is a separate workbook to begin or continue the process.

One Powerful Key

To increase your ability to see in the spiritual realm here is one powerful but simple key.... When you go to bed and the room is dark or at least semi- dark , spend about five or ten minutes laying still and studying the air or atmosphere around you. There are things that occupy this "empty" space, we just have to pay attention. Also upon waking do the same thing. We choose these times because of the quietness and lack of natural distractions. This is one way to follow the instructions of this verse in Corinthians.

So we fix our eyes not on what is seen, but on what is unseen, since what is seen is temporary, but what is unseen is eternal. (2 Corinthians 4:18)

Developing Your Ability to Hear God and All your Spiritual Senses

Being led of the spirit is a huge part of entering into the supernatural things of God. We want to be like our Lord and only say what we hear the Father say, but to do that we actually have to hear Him. This is yet another part of walking in the supernatural and is also very important. The Lord says...

My sheep hear My voice, and I know them, and they follow Me. (John 10:27)

We have to be aware that God does speak to us and we have the capacity to hear Him. He wants us to hear Him. There are many ways that God speaks to us, such as through His spirit, in the Word, by prophetic word, by an inner witness or knowing, by His still, small voice as well as others. Listen for Him and listen to Him. As you study the Word ask Him to speak to you and make it plain. He will give you the desires of your heart. There are also several good resources to learn to hear God's voice and develop in this.

Praying in Tongues

In the same way, the Spirit helps us in our weakness. We do not know what we ought to pray for, but the Spirit himself intercedes for us through wordless groans.   (Romans 8:26)

Praying in the spirit builds up our spirit man and helps increase our faith. (Rom. 12:6; Jude 1:20; Mark 9:23; Matt. 9:29).

Praying in tongues is allowing the manifestation of the Holy Spirit in you and in your circumstances. (1 Cor. 14:2, 14).

We need to lay hold of Divine secrets. Especially if we want to receive the things of Heaven.

"For he who speaks in a 'tongue' addresses God, not man; no one understands him; he is talking of divine secrets in the Spirit" (1 Corinthians 14:2)

If you pray in tongues for extended periods of time it will open up the things of the spiritual realm. If you are seeking spiritual gifts, revelation, if you are doing spiritual warfare, or building up your spirit praying without ceasing, or praying in tongues will cause amazing breakthrough.

Engaging the Kingdom

Sit quietly and still, relax and pray quietly in tongues. Be as still as you can so you can feel the effect it has on your spirit. Try different amounts of prayer time and journal it.

** This is something that most people have to discipline themselves to do. Don't be surprised or discouraged if it takes a little time to feel the results of doing this.

8

FIRST IN THE SPIRIT

A Few Things to Remember...

Thy Will be Done

As we go and move into the spiritual realm we must always keep in mind that we have a divine purpose in going. Although the experiences are far beyond anything that the natural mind can process, our main focus is doing the will of the Father.

Jesus gave them this answer: "Very truly I tell you, the Son can do nothing by himself; he can do only what he sees his Father doing, because whatever the Father does the Son also does. (John 5:19)

Steps of Faith

Another thing to remember as we seek to see this manifested as reality is that everything we do, we do by faith. These are all steps of faith that develop and expand the more we engage and the more we exercise our faith. It's the same principle as the scripture that tells us to make an effort to study and learn the Word.

Study to shew thyself approved unto God, a workman that needeth not to be ashamed, rightly dividing the word of truth. (2 Timothy 2:15)

God does not (usually) give us this knowledge without our participation. We take steps that bring us to this greater manifestation. We make an effort.

Come near to God and he will come near to you. Wash your hands, you sinners, and purify your hearts, you double-minded. (James 4:8)

Soak Your Journey in Prayer

"...you have not, because you ask not..." (James 4:2)

As we engage the things of God, continually ask Holy Spirit for guidance and direction. He is the one who leads us into all truth. He is the teacher and comforter. (John 16:13)

Be aware!

Awareness of God, awareness of what is going on around you in the natural and in the spiritual is a marker to help you in this journey. You are venturing into places and new experiences and your awareness will help to bring greater fulfillment. Also be aware that...

1. God will help you.

2. If it was quick and easy with no effort required, everyone would have this.

3. There will be dry times and the enemy will try to discourage you. Don't give in!

4. The reward is well worth the sacrifice. Even "tasting" this can be life changing.

The Lord's Instructions...First in the Spirit

When the Lord gave me the mandate to teach this for end times ministry to the body of Christ, he gave me instructions and also told me how this would begin to be manifested in the lives of those who desired to be a part of this. The Lord first told me that there would be two phases to this. He said that the first step was that as I taught this, people would begin to be caught away and have third Heaven experiences by being caught away in the spirit. He said this would happen before they would be physically translocated to different geographic regions of the world to do what God has for them to do. This is a key part. This supernatural movement is for the plans and purposes of God.

Engaging the Kingdom - Coming Before the Throne

As with the majority of the exercises / engagements we do, we will begin by getting into our position of prayer and stillness before God. (Just like the previous Engaging the Kingdom exercises) By faith, in your imagination see yourself traveling or moving up and into the heavens and coming up before the Throne of God.

When we arrive, kneel and lift your hands and begin to worship God. As you do this, come into agreement with the other worshippers and the angels around you who are also worshipping God.

As you worship, let your desire for Him be unrestrained. Allow and feel His light surrounding you to enter into you. Pull His light and love and presence into you by your desire for Him.

Do this for a period of between fifteen minutes to an hour and then journal the experience. Then repeat this journey several times and also journal that as well. As you do this moving in and out of the Kingdom and into the Throne room, you will find that your awareness will increase and you will notice more of what is going on. The reason we go in and out (15 min. – 1 hour and repeat) is because we are training ourselves to move in and out as a normal function of who we are in Christ. When the Lord tells us to go somewhere, we won't have to try to work up some faith to do it. We will already be living in that place of faith.

Write down your observations

**If you are doing these exercises / engagements as a group after each journey, compare notes. What did everyone see. Feel or experience? Were there things in common that everyone saw? Perhaps everyone saw a huge angel or a living creature or a doorway etc..

Engaging the Kingdom - A Visit With the Lord

Pick a place in Heaven. (Such as the Sea of Glass or the Garden or The Library Room or Hall of Faith) and ask the Lord to meet you there. Just a simple prayer like "Lord I want to spend some time with you. Will you meet me in the Garden so I can speak to you there?"

Now, get into the position of prayer and stillness and by faith ascend into that place. See and speak with the Lord and ask Him questions. Ask Him among other things, How He feels about you and what He thinks about you. Also ask Him to talk to you about your purpose in the Kingdom. If you are in a group study, ask the Lord about His plans for this group and if He has specific words for anyone. Talk about what the Lord tells you.

1.Lord, What do you think and feel about me?

2. Lord, Tell me about my purpose in the Kingdom.

3.Lord, do you have any words for the group?

Engaging the Kingdom – The Cloud of Witnesses

Tell the Lord that you would like to engage Heaven. Ask Him to allow interaction with the cloud of witnesses. Is there a favorite Bible character that you admire or relate to? Perhaps someone that if you had the chance you like to pose questions to? The cloud of witnesses is all around us. They are most happy and willing to help in any way that they can to bring about God's purpose in your life.

You know that you may have already spoken to them in the spirit realm. Your spirit is already seated in the Heavenly places! Choose the one you would like to visit with and ask him or her two questions. Record the highlights of the conversation below. Also ask them to give you a scripture. Ask for them to take you into a Bible story that they were a part of and explain to you about the event.

Engaging the Kingdom – Our Comfort Zones

In becoming accustomed to the spiritual realm, many times even the idea of it can seem daunting. We are blazing new trails so to speak so we can be very much out of our "comfort zone." So for this engagement we are going to stay in our comfort zone (sort of) and yet leave it at the same time. (we normally feel safe and comfortable in our home)

Praying over your home

Begin this exercise by sitting in your prayer chair or by laying down or whatever happens to be your most comfortable prayer position. Then say out loud "I'm going to get up and walk around the house and pray." Then get up from your position and walk a particular path through your home ten times and pray over the house and environment as you go, always taking the same route.

After you have done this, go back to your prayer chair / position and relax and pray softly in tongues for ten to fifteen minutes. Then after you are sufficiently relaxed, say in your imagination "I'm going to get up and walk around the house and pray." And then see yourself getting up and going on the same prayer path you just took in the natural realm. This is one thing that you can do every night in your home. It will give you the opportunity to bring the atmosphere of Heaven into your home while at the same time you will be engaging the spiritual realm. This constant engagement of the same place, a place that you know well and feel secure in will allow you to begin to shift from the natural realm to the spiritual with full awareness of being in the spiritual realm, as you pray.

** One thing to note here is that as you have more awareness in the spirit, as you walk through your home you may see things that are not there in the natural realm. Things like curtains hanging in the air, Perhaps a piece of furniture that isn't there in the natural or sometimes doors that are not there in the natural. These things are the spiritual environment of your home. If you see things look gloomy at all start worshipping the lord more in your home.

Since you will be praying anyway, really make it count. Soak and saturate every little piece of your home with prayer. Also record anything significant you sense, see or find.

Engaging the Kingdom – Venturing out

All of us have people in our lives who really need prayer. Some need healing and some need salvation and some we don't know what they need but everyone needs prayer. So ask the Holy Spirit to tell you who to pray for and then go get ready to pray.

Now go to your prayer position and see yourself going to that person to pray for them. You may see yourself flying there or even driving a car. When you get to where they are, you might speak with them and you might not. Most of the time they don't ever know that you are there. Sometimes they will feel the power of your prayer and may react to it.

If you pray in this manner for someone who needs healing for instance, you may see incredible manifestations of God's healing power. You see, in the spirit realm, you do not carry all that doubt and unbelief with you. You know beyond a shadow of doubt that all things are indeed possible and when you pray in the spirit you pray with exponential faith. You have an awareness in the spirit that you don't normally see in the natural.

Write the name of the person the Lord has told you to pray for and what their issue is . (If you can) Then as you go pray for them keep a record. Is the situation changing"

Engaging the Kingdom - Worshipping God in the Spirit

Music as a Door

We know that the Lord inhabits the praises of His people. (Psalms 22:3) If there is one thing that we absolutely should be doing it is worshipping the Lord. Worship takes you places that nothing else will. Worship also provides an excellent covering for warfare as well. Be a worshipper!

Choose some anointed worship music to worship with. For this one you can sit, stand or lay, but I recommend that you do this in every possible way. Let's say that you are standing and worshipping along with the song. Now close your eyes and see that you are now worshipping with a great throng of people. Worship for a few minutes in the spirit and then return and worship in the natural. Keep going back and forth as you worship. The atmosphere of worship will allow you greater access and the fact that you are moving back and forth will train you to move in the Kingdom realm.

As always journal your experiences and you will see increase.

The Importance of Journaling

In all of these engaging the Kingdom exercises you are given a space to record your experiences. The space provided should not be enough for the amount of spiritual activity that you do. The journaling does several things. First, it gives you a clear record of the events in your life. This way you will have them for encouragement or teaching or comparison etc.. The next thing it does is it signifies a step of faith. When you get your pen and notebook out and set it where it can be seen and used, you are telling the Lord "Lord I believe you are going to give me something to write in it." Third, You are training yourself to remember and pay attention. The fact that you are doing this will cause you to notice all the little things that might otherwise slip past you.

9

PHYSICAL TRANSLOCATION

Philip's Translocation in Acts Chapter 8

26 Now an angel of the Lord spoke to Philip, saying, "Arise and go toward the south along the road which goes down from Jerusalem to Gaza." This is desert. 27 So he arose and went. And behold, a man of Ethiopia, a eunuch of great authority under Candace the queen of the Ethiopians, who had charge of all her treasury, and had come to Jerusalem to worship, 28 was returning. And sitting in his chariot, he was reading Isaiah the prophet. 29 Then the Spirit said to Philip, "Go near and overtake this chariot."

30 So Philip ran to him, and heard him reading the prophet Isaiah, and said, "Do you understand what you are reading?"

31 And he said, "How can I, unless someone guides me?" And he asked Philip to come up and sit with him. 32 The place in the Scripture which he read was this:

"He was led as a sheep to the slaughter; And as a lamb before its shearer is silent, So He opened not His mouth. 33 In His humiliation His justice was taken away, And who will declare His generation? For His life is taken from the earth."

34 So the eunuch answered Philip and said, "I ask you, of whom does the prophet say this, of himself or of some other man?" 35 Then Philip opened his mouth, and

beginning at this Scripture, preached Jesus to him. 36 Now as they went down the road, they came to some water. And the eunuch said, "See, here is water. What hinders me from being baptized?"

37 Then Philip said, "If you believe with all your heart, you may."

And he answered and said, "I believe that Jesus Christ is the Son of God."[c]

38 So he commanded the chariot to stand still. And both Philip and the eunuch went down into the water, and he baptized him. 39 Now when they came up out of the water, the Spirit of the Lord caught Philip away, so that the eunuch saw him no more; and he went on his way rejoicing. 40 But Philip was found at Azotus. And passing through, he preached in all the cities till he came to Caesarea.

The Purposes of God

Right away in this passage we see that an angel of the Lord brought the instruction for Philip to do this ministry assignment. We also know that even the Lord Jesus Himself said...

Jesus gave them this answer: "Very truly I tell you, the Son can do nothing by himself; he can do only what he sees his Father doing, because whatever the Father does the Son also does. (John 5:19)

This is a key in moving in the things of God. To stay safely in the center of God's will and not seek another way. I would like to stress this because there are many today just as there were in the past that are tempted to bring in mixture to the supernatural things of God.

God is more concerned about our character than He is about our gifts and ministry. He would rather that we be Christ-like than talented. Many people grow weary of the process because it only goes as fast as we are willing to submit to God. If we hold on to areas that we need to let go of, it prolongs the sanctification process and sometimes the ministry gifts such as spiritual sight or supernatural translation are left "on hold."

Rather than acknowledge that God is doing a greater work, there are many who seek to "supplement" God's way with certain new age practices. This is particularly true of things like supernatural sight and translation and translocation for some reason.

Don't fall into that trap. Just seek the Lord and He will bring the manifestation of all the wonderful things we desire for our lives.

But seek ye first the kingdom of God, and his righteousness; and all these things shall be added unto you. (Matthew 6:33)

Mike's Testimony...

One day I happened to "catch" an angel going somewhere and I stopped him and asked him to help me. He asked me what I needed, so I told him that I want to see better in the spirit. The angel showed me what my eyes looked like in the spiritual realm, (not good) and then told me that my eyes were damaged from all the garbage I had put into them over the years. Then he said that the Lord could heal them.

This encounter really confirmed something for me. I 'd had a Christian friend that was telling me that there were much better ways to see in the spirit than what I was teaching. He said something about me learning to vibrate at different frequencies. However, an angel told me my eyes needed to be sanctified and healed...Who should I listen to? The Lord of course. We may indeed vibrate at a certain frequency when we are in prolonged worship but we don't worship with the goal being to "vibrate." We worship God because He is worthy of our worship.

The thing we need to do is to stay in faith. Listen intently to the Lord's voice and be ready to move. The Lord is the one directing our steps and paths (even the ancient paths) and if we want to be a part of this we need to be aware of that.

What we are doing is making ourselves accessible to the Lord. And just like the spiritual manifestation, the physical is no different in the fact that it may not be easy at first. Most of us have little or no manifestation or knowledge of it when we start, so it can be easy to grow impatient or weary. When we talk of accessing portals and doors or ancient pathways, we are really talking about developing a discipline as well. This is also a time of developing your spiritual senses at the same time. It's all a part of the journey.

More Steps of Faith...

As with the previous section, these areas of engagement are steps of faith that we take to see it manifested. Just like in divine healing or anything else God does, we make ourselves available, take a step of faith and then watch God move.

The exercises presented all through this workbook are not one size fits all formulas but rather different ways that we have used to engage with God that have been fruitful. The Lord has given us steps to take, but under the care and guidance of the Holy Spirit.

Do You Know How Real This Is?

It bolsters our faith when we hear the amazing testimonies of what God is doing now all across the world. And knowing that He is no respecter of persons lets you know that He will use you as well.

A Few More Testimonies

We already mentioned Brother Grubbs who God used mightily in this way, but there are many, many more. We will mention the instances that are shared openly as testimonies.

Billye Brimm – Anointed minister of the Gospel: She spoke to Gloria Copeland on her television program and told an account of a Russian Pastor whom the Lord translocated supernaturally for years so that he could preach at another church that was several hours away. Because of her great love for this family, she decided to purchase a car for them so to make their lives easier. The minute she handed the car keys to the pastor, supernatural translocation ceased. He was saddened and she was as well for having given him the keys.

Jeff Jansen – Pastor and revivalist: Author of the popular book "Glory Rising" He was supposed to speak at a conference in Ohio one Friday, Saturday and Sunday, but had to inform the hosting church that he could not make it until Saturday because he had obligations to be at his home church in Tennessee. That Saturday when he showed up at the church in Ohio, he apologized for not being able to come the previous night. The Pastor as well as everyone else didn't understand. They told Jeff that he was indeed there that Friday and Jeff insisted he wasn't. The pastor then found over thirty people that Jeff had prayed for the previous night and even had a video clip of him waving from the balcony when they acknowledged him. Jeff realized that God had done something unusual and spectacular. How about that?! God not only supernaturally translocated him that night, but allowed him to be in two places at once, in Ohio and Tennessee!

David Hogan – Evangelist and Missionary to Mexico: David tells this amazing account. David said that he was at Guillermo Maldonado's church in Miami, standing in the green room just waiting with his family before the service was to start. There were several pastors from all over South America who had come to Miami for the event and they were also in the greenroom. As they waited, one of the pastors from South America walked over to David and greeted him warmly and said thank you so much for coming to our church earlier in the year. David told the man he was sorry but he must be mistaken because he had never been there. The man insisted that David had not only been there but also played the guitar and sang!. David responded that he must be mistaken because he doesn't do "song services. "After a few minutes of trying to convince each other, the man took out his cell phone and played a video for David.. "Are you telling me that that's not you playing the guitar and singing in this video/" David looked and indeed it was him.

It gets better. The date was the same day he was doing a conference in Germany and they later found out that he had also delivered a truckload of lumber to a church in Mexico on the same day!

There is testimony after testimony of God translocating people all over the world to preach and pray and heal the sick and any number of other things. The ones that share openly these types of testimonies are people like Dr. James Maloney, Bobby Conner, Bob Jones, Patricia King, Dennis Walker, John Paul Jackson and more. This is not being done in secret but rather the Lord is openly doing these signs and wonders in this age.

Supernatural Time Travel

Can God move us through time? Of course He can. Time exists in God and He can bend it however He desires to. There are several examples in the Bible of God either supernaturally suspending time or moving people through time. He still does this.

So the sun stood still, and the moon stopped, till the nation avenged itself on its enemies, as it is written in the Book of Jashar. The sun stopped in the middle of the sky and delayed going down about a full day. (Joshua 10:13)

God held time almost a full day.

John the revelator was taken into the future to see the final things to come. He describes in great detail the things he sees in the book of Revelation.

Bruce's Testimony...

I was sharing with my friend John about what God was teaching me about translation by faith before we were to take a drive together from Edmonds Washington to Spokane. And so I told John "Let's pray." Now this trip was a five to six hour trip under good circumstances if you were able to go the speed limit. John's car was an old car that ran by faith. And so we prayed and I asked the Lord for my first lesson in translation by faith. We put on the song "This is the Air I Breathe" and we started out. We just started out and began worshipping God. About halfway stopped for lunch and filled up with gas and continued on the journey. When we got to our destination, we looked at the time and realized that we had made the trip in under two hours. It was about an hour and twenty minutes. God had supernaturally transported us.

I told the Lord "I don't get it Father." And the Lord told me "In your mind the shortest distance between two points is a straight line." And He folded the line over and said "the shortest distance is already being there."

Engaging the Kingdom – Traveling Through Time

The Lord holds time in the palm of His hand. If we can grasp the significance of this, it will change the way we pray and believe for these things. There will never be that gut wrenching finality of "It's too late." There is a scripture that talks about the Lord redeeming the days. We can believe for this and lay hold of this by faith. And just like in the previous testimony, God will do for any one of you what He does for me. He is no respecter of persons.

Lay hold of the previous testimony and exercise your own faith for similar experiences.

As you start your day and move about, driving to work or to church or other places you might go, lay hands on your vehicle and make a declaration similar to this. "In Jesus' name I release you to travel supernaturally and move through time and space." Now believe that God will begin to do this and teach you about this aspect of it. Pick one particular drive that you do the most (such as to work every day) and keep a log of the time it should take to make the drive and the recorded time that it actually took. If you expect this enough to actually do this the Lord will honor that faith. He is the one who is training us in these things after all.

Engaging the Kingdom – Already Being There

What is faster than accelerated travel from one place to another? You already know. Already being there.

For in him we live, and move, and have our being; as certain also of your own poets have said, For we are also his offspring. (Acts 17:28)

Take the previous exercise and rather than asking the Lord to accelerate or slow time, ask him to immediately translocate you to the place you are traveling to. Take at least 3-5 minutes and focus and imagine moving to that place. Imagination is a powerful door.

Remember, God is doing this in the earth today and we must ask! The Bible says we have not because we ask not. Let's ask and believe and take steps of faith!

Mike's Testimony...

I write my own accounts in notebooks because the nice journals got to be too cost prohibitive to keep using. But If I were to fill out this particular form, one of my entries would look like this...

Date Wed. 25 Jul 12 Place Carmel IN. USA __ to Somewhere in N.E. USA_____

Result Prayed all night- got up and stepped outside at 4am- found myself standing in front of a church that was having a conference - I spoke to one of the speakers and prayed with 2 women – came back vibrating with electricity going through my body.

You should always write a result. Even if it is "nothing extreme" write it down. Very often as God begins to teach you these things, you may experience nothing but you may also experience things like a powerful presence of God, vibrations or electricity, a heavy feeling like a warm blanket etc.. Write everything down and look for increase.

Engaging the Kingdom – Human Touch

For this exercise, think of the type of place that you might go that you would minister with a "human touch" as well. (Where you actually touch someone physically) This might be a hospital or a nursing home or anywhere that you would want to touch people to help them realize that they are loved.

Even in this physical aspect, it is easier it seems to start out in a quiet, isolated place where you would not be disturbed or distracted. Once you do this more you will see what your own journey looks like and can make your adjustments with the help of the Holy Spirit.

On a practical note... If you are asking the Lord in the middle of the night to take you to a hospital to pray for people, don't be dressed in your pajamas! Have proper clothing on and be ready to go. If you are translocating to a church service, put your church clothes on. (whatever that might be for you)

You see it is a step of faith to even make yourself ready for this journey!

Engaging the Kingdom – A Common Place

This time pick a place that you are very familiar with. A place where you know the look of the place, the smells, the feel etc.. Get in the position that best allows you to engage. If you are seated where you are, be seated in your imagination there. The more connected your imagination is in these engagements, the faster this will happen. (Of course it goes without saying that everything we do must be under the direct supervision of the Holy Spirit.)

**If you are in a group, try to pick a spot that everyone is familiar with. Even if you must get up physically from where you are and go to a common area to have a new location please do so. There is power in agreement. Something special happens when you have everyone pulling the same direction and aspiring to a common goal.

Engaging the Kingdom – Ask Holy Spirit !!!

Of course! We should be asking the Holy Spirit continually as He guides us. For this exercise, ask Him to move us to a place that He has chosen and give us a mission or purpose there.

Record the Holy Spirit's Assignment and Result.

The Reality

The reality is that many of you going through this workbook and doing these things are already experiencing miraculous things from the Lord. Whether it is signs and wonders or the flashes of light that can happen when your spiritual eyes open or even already being translated or translocated, God is preparing you and has already given you the desire. The desire for Him, His Kingdom and His will. This workbook is a jumping off place for greater increase and manifestation. Exercises and engagements that help us to exercise our faith that are tested and have been used by God.

So these next few engaging the Kingdom exercises will be designed by you and the Holy Spirit, making them unique to your heart and desire with the passions that the Lord has given you, written into the instructions. Write them out and do them! I have a strong feeling that the ones you write out specifically for yourself may yield the greatest fruit of all!

Make them specific to your calling. If you are called to minister to children, make the journey about children somehow. Or the same could apply to the homeless or those in prisons or any other thing on your heart.

10

THE REALITY IS, YOU ARE LIGHT!

This is certainly one of the most important revelations to lay hold of if you desire to walk in translation by faith. We have understood from an allegorical and metaphorical standpoint the mentions in the Bible about us being light or children of the light etc.. But the Lord is shedding *new* light and revelation on this subject, and this Godly revelation is being validated by the most brilliant minds in the scientific community. It seems that science is finally catching up to the Word and we see that we truly are light!

I'm going to unpack some of the foundational revelation that the Lord has given me concerning light, so let me start closer to the beginning.

We have authority over the physics of light in the natural realm...

I have given you dominion over the works of my hand.   **(Psalm 8:6)**

We are created in the image of God, who is light. We are a greater light than created light because we are part of his body. Just as the scripture above states, we have authority over all created things including light.

The Word of the Lord

At the beginning of 2016 I asked the Lord *"What are you saying for this year?"* And the Lord spoke to me and said *"This is the year of Isaiah sixty for my people."*

I was extremely excited that the Lord had given me *that* word. You see, for the last several years the Lord has been teaching me about light. To say that these revelations were life altering is a understatement, and the fact that He is releasing them now to the church for 2016 is quite a powerful sign.

Isaiah Sixty

Arise, shine; for thy light is come, and the glory of the LORD is risen upon thee.

2 For, behold, the darkness shall cover the earth, and gross darkness the people: but the LORD shall arise upon thee, and his glory shall be seen upon thee.

3 And the Gentiles shall come to thy light, and kings to the brightness of thy rising.

4 Lift up thine eyes round about, and see: all they gather themselves together, they come to thee: thy sons shall come from far, and thy daughters shall be nursed at thy side.

5 Then thou shalt see, and flow together, and thine heart shall fear, and be enlarged; because the abundance of the sea shall be converted unto thee, the forces of the Gentiles shall come unto thee.

6 The multitude of camels shall cover thee, the dromedaries of Midian and Ephah; all they from Sheba shall come: they shall bring gold and incense; and they shall shew forth the praises of the LORD.

7 All the flocks of Kedar shall be gathered together unto thee, the rams of Nebaioth shall minister unto thee: they shall come up with acceptance on mine altar, and I will glorify the house of my glory.

8 Who are these that fly as a cloud, and as the doves to their windows?

9 Surely the isles shall wait for me, and the ships of Tarshish first, to bring thy sons from far, their silver and their gold with them, unto the name of the LORD thy God, and to the Holy One of Israel, because he hath glorified thee.

10 And the sons of strangers shall build up thy walls, and their kings shall minister unto thee: for in my wrath I smote thee, but in my favour have I had mercy on thee.

¹¹ Therefore thy gates shall be open continually; they shall not be shut day nor night; that men may bring unto thee the forces of the Gentiles, and that their kings may be brought.

¹² For the nation and kingdom that will not serve thee shall perish; yea, those nations shall be utterly wasted.

¹³ The glory of Lebanon shall come unto thee, the fir tree, the pine tree, and the box together, to beautify the place of my sanctuary; and I will make the place of my feet glorious.

¹⁴ The sons also of them that afflicted thee shall come bending unto thee; and all they that despised thee shall bow themselves down at the soles of thy feet; and they shall call thee; The city of the LORD, The Zion of the Holy One of Israel.

¹⁵ Whereas thou has been forsaken and hated, so that no man went through thee, I will make thee an eternal excellency, a joy of many generations.

¹⁶ Thou shalt also suck the milk of the Gentiles, and shalt suck the breast of kings: and thou shalt know that I the LORD am thy Saviour and thy Redeemer, the mighty One of Jacob.

¹⁷ For brass I will bring gold, and for iron I will bring silver, and for wood brass, and for stones iron: I will also make thy officers peace, and thine exactors righteousness.

¹⁸ Violence shall no more be heard in thy land, wasting nor destruction within thy borders; but thou shalt call thy walls Salvation, and thy gates Praise.

¹⁹ The sun shall be no more thy light by day; neither for brightness shall the moon give light unto thee: but the LORD shall be unto thee an everlasting light, and thy God thy glory.

²⁰ Thy sun shall no more go down; neither shall thy moon withdraw itself: for the LORD shall be thine everlasting light, and the days of thy mourning shall be ended.

²¹ Thy people also shall be all righteous: they shall inherit the land for ever, the branch of my planting, the work of my hands, that I may be glorified.

²² A little one shall become a thousand, and a small one a strong nation: I the LORD will hasten it in his time.

Read this chapter a few times and let it sink in. Meditate upon it. This is the word of the Lord! This is what God is calling you to walk in.

Visitation, Revelation and Activation

One of the most important aspects of Isaiah sixty is right at the very beginning.

Arise! Shine! For thy light has come.

Arise is the key here. This is something that you must do. You arise! It is a step of faith. God has given us an instruction to take a step of faith. You say you're not sure exactly how you do that? **Do *something.***

This is a very common thing to those who have a lifestyle of seeking God. Taking steps of faith that bring a manifestation of spiritual things. Many call these steps "prophetic gestures" or something similar to that. These are physical "gestures" or actions, that represent a step towards engagement with the spiritual dimension.

This is a prevalent thing all throughout the scriptures. When you see someone contending for or believing for a miracle or intervention from God, they receive some type of instruction. Very often the things God asks us to do look like foolishness, especially in the eyes of the world. Take for example the story of Naaman in Second Kings chapter five. Naaman had leprosy and went to Elisha to be healed. Instead of doing some spectacular thing, Elisha sent a servant to give him a simple instruction.

9 So Naaman went with his horses and chariots and stopped at the door of Elisha's house. 10 Elisha sent a messenger to say to him, "Go, wash yourself seven times in the Jordan, and your flesh will be restored and you will be cleansed." 11 But Naaman went away angry and said, "I thought that he would surely come out to me and stand and call on the name of the Lord his God, wave his hand over the spot and cure me of my leprosy. 12 Are not Abana and Pharpar, the rivers of Damascus, better than all the waters of Israel? Couldn't I wash in them and be cleansed?" So he turned and went off in a rage. (2 Kings 5:9-12)

Had Naaman not been provoked later to at least follow this simple instruction he may very well have missed his miracle. It's the same for us. Many times in conference settings or Walking in the Supernatural Schools or similar settings, we might hear an instruction… *"Lift your hands."* or *"Stand up."* or *"Say I receive it."* If we are not sensitive to the Spirit we can dismiss simple instructions such as these as unimportant, when the reality is that God is the one speaking.

So as the Lord began to teach me this revelation, He said *"Arise, shine!"* So I stood up! **Obedience.** I would rather err stepping out in faith than do nothing. Then the Lord told me *"The glory of the Lord is risen upon you."* Then as the Lord was talking to me about Isaiah sixty, He began to remind me of the things He had already taught me.

Here are some important keys the Lord has given me…

A Visitation

A few years ago I was speaking at a conference and when I asked the Lord for revelation to share, I was caught away in the spirit. As I stood there before the Lord, He had me pull apart my garment of flesh, much like the way Superman pulled back his clothing to reveal the "S" under his clothing. When I pulled back the garment, intense light beamed out. I started to let my garment of flesh go back into place when the Lord said *"No! Disrobe from your garment of flesh,"* and so I did. And when I did, I was standing there as a being of light! I looked behind me and I saw the garment of my flesh laying on the ground much like clothing cast aside might appear. As I stood there before the Lord as a being of light, the Lord said *"You tell my people that this is who they really are."*

When I came back to the natural realm, because of the magnitude of the revelation I had just received, I asked the Lord for a confirmation and He gave me this verse...

For God hath not given us the spirit of fear; but of power, and of love, and of a sound mind. (2 Timothy 1:7)

Confirming Visitations

Just one month later I was conducting a conference and a friend of mine, Brother Sadhu came and was telling me of his visitations with Moses and Abraham. After he had shared with me concerning his visitation, he said Moses told him "Oh, and tell Bruce to study light. Because the key to what the Lord has told him to walk in is the study of light." He was referring to translation by faith.

Again, just one month later I was doing a conference in Sydney, Australia with Brother Sadhu and Brother Neville Johnson.

Before the conference I was in my room praying, and suddenly I was not in the room anymore, but I was in a huge cave. And there was an opening before me and what appeared to be a massive sun going down at sunset. Immediately I knew that the sunset was speaking about the end of the age. And the cave I was in was Christ, the solid rock. I was in the cleft of the rock. And as I stood there marveling at this sight, I noticed movement beside me and I looked and there stood Elijah.

I asked him why he was here. He said *"The Lord sent me to teach you how a man can go from the natural realm to eternity without seeing death."* Now this was a very powerful thing that was happening because the Lord had *already* told me that this was the Elijah generation! And the Word confirms that at the end of the age there will be a people that will come forth in the spirit and power of Elijah.

Elijah said to me *"Watch."* And he stuck out his hand and it turned to light. And he looked at me and said *"Go ahead."* And so I stuck my hand out and began *trying* to do what he had done but it wasn't working so good. Elijah started laughing, he said *"No. Remember what the Lord has already taught you. You are already a being of light. Quit striving with your intellect and quit striving with your flesh. Just become."*

So I stuck out my hand again and this time it became light. Elijah said *"Good. Practice."* And so I began to practice.

More Confirmations

I also need to mention that one year earlier on Rosh Hashanah, the Lord had given me a key made of *light* that's purpose was to open portals and doorways, access points to traverse spiritually or geographically.

Now I looked and there is Elijah holding my key of light. I was thinking *'How did you get that?"* He said to me *"Put out your hand."* And so I put out my hand which was now light, and he set the key in my hand and it dissolved into me. I asked him what had just happened and he responded *"You are the same frequency of light. **You are the key!"***

Elijah had more to teach me and said *"Follow me."* And then Elijah walked through the wall! I tried to follow him and walked *into* the wall and Elijah laughed again. I then remembered the things that I had been taught and came to a place of rest and stepped through the wall also. However the mantle that I had on was caught on the wall and prevented me from moving forward. Elijah then said *"Leave that mantle. It is "second day" it's time to walk in the new mantle that is being released in this generation."*

Yet More Confirmations and Revelation

I told the Lord *"Lord, in the mouths of two or three witnesses."* The following day Ezekiel came. Ezekiel was standing before me with three mantles. The Lord had brought confirmation.

This *revelation* of light, that we are beings of light, is of tantamount importance. So important in fulfilling the mandate the Lord has given me (which is teaching translation by faith) that He is providing numerous instructions all on this subject of light, by the Lord himself *and* his prophets, confirming everything in multiple ways. I would say He *really* wants us to get this.

Take hold of everything you have just read and meditate on it. Think about these encounters and instructions. Now realize that God is no respecter of persons! What He has done for me He will do for you and in fact that is what this is all about. Raising *you* up to walk in the reality of translation by faith!

Finding Light

The Lord told me to study light. As I obeyed that instruction He began to break open the revelation so that I could walk in it. **Get in the Word**. Find as many references as you can concerning light and it's relation to us. (as we have been talking about)

Write the verse and ask Holy Spirit to give you revelation and write it down. Even if it is only a word or two, begin in faith and watch Him also tutor and train you.

Believing The Impossible

The things that we talk about in this workbook and this chapter in particular, are beyond the pale for most Christians. Many would consider this science fiction-like, as most have had no instruction or revelation in this area. But this is how awesome our God is...He has given scientists the ability to prove the truth of the Word and the revelation.

Light, The Miraculous and Quantum Physics

Quantum physics is what is used by scientists to understand the properties of solids, atoms, nuclei, sub-nuclear particles and light. It is the branch of physics that deals with the atomic and sub atomic building blocks of our world (s).

Once you have even a very basic knowledge of this field, you begin to understand that many of the things we have previously dismissed as being impossible, have been scientifically proven to be possible. Quantum physics demystifies some of the things we have not previously understood and creates new "mysteries" to be unraveled.

Not to take this into a deep scientific discourse, I would just like to show you a few things that scientists have proven. First of all, we have learned that (created) light travels at 186,00 miles per second. If we travel at the speed of light, time stands still. If you can move at the speed of light you can step out of time and into eternity. If we travel faster than the speed of light, we can go backward in time. In the quantum world, there is no past, present or future. They exist simultaneously.

There is something in quantum physics called the split–light theory. Scientists have shown that light is intelligent. It has a consciousness. In experiments, a beam of light was split in two and as the beam traveled out a certain distance, the photons came back together. It "healed" itself and became a single beam again!

Also through science, we know that atoms that make up everything including things that appear solid, are made up of over ninety-nine percent empty space. The building blocks of our world when taken to their smallest parts are virtually empty space. This gives us a bit of understanding of how one seemingly solid object could possibly pass through another.

We have also learned that observation and intention change the way atoms behave. An electron when not being observed, behaves like a wave yet when it is being observed behaves as a solid. We also know that the intention of the one observing the function can change its direction. In other words if you are observing particles moving in a clockwise direction and you observe them and think about them moving counter clockwise, they will change directions to match your expectations.

And broken into the most basic form, everything is light. (energy) *We really are light!*

I know these few examples have probably created more questions than they have answered but that's a good thing! Study this aspect of light and quantum physics, and understand that God created things this way!

If you have an interest to explore this further, Dr. David Van Koevering has some incredible revelation concerning quantum physics and is indeed one of the most respected scientists in this field and he is also a believer.

Do a Quick Study

Do a little research and come up with five things that quantum physics has proven that seemingly defy our natural thinking / reasoning.

Breaking Down Barriers of Doubt and Unbelief

One of the great blessings of quantum science is that it helps remove the objections that one's mind might try to interject as we learn to lay hold of "the impossible." Quantum physics has shown that not only is it possible, **it is the reality.** (The supernatural)

Stepping Out in Faith

After the Lord began to teach me about the fact that we are light and that this was a vital key (a literal key) that we must lay hold of, I began to follow His instructions to practice. Every morning when I get up I dedicate my members to Him and His use. Then I close my eyes and see myself divesting myself of my physical body and stepping out as a being of light. I do this every day. You see that you can hear an instruction like this and you can give it a mental ascent and say "Yes, that's nice" or "Yes, that's a great idea" and never lay hold of the reality and manifestation of it. But if you take the revelation for yourself and really embrace it and take steps of faith such as this, you will see the manifestation of light in your own life and others will see it as well.

Encouraging Testimonies

The Lord has shown me through testimonies also that these exercises, or steps of faith are bearing great fruit. Many times in churches I visit, I have been told things like "When you were up there speaking you were literally glowing" or "We took pictures during the service and everyone looks fine except you. You look like just a big light!" As you begin to hear testimonies such as these you understand that God is truly doing an obvious work. This is not something hidden, but something that people are seeing with their natural eyes. This manifestation is like what is described in Matthew chapter seventeen that the Lord experienced on the mount of Transfiguration.

1 After six days Jesus took with him Peter, James and John the brother of James, and led them up a high mountain by themselves. 2 There he was transfigured before them. His face shone like the sun, and his clothes became as white as the light. 3 Just then there appeared before them Moses and Elijah, talking with Jesus. (Matthew 17:1-3)

Like what Peter, James and John saw, this is not a mystical experience that people are seeing by faith but a literal seeing of a literal manifestation of light. This is what God is bringing us into. If you can get this revelation on light, it will be life changing.

When you walk in the light as He is in the light, you will change every environment you enter. As He is, so are we in this world. As light we don't fear darkness. The only thing faster than light is darkness. Because as soon as light comes darkness is gone! Christians should not fear the devil. When we show up demons will try to hide. The light that you are, the light that you carry exposes darkness and they don't like it. You don't have to fear.

As this light manifests it will change your world. The scriptures say...

... Gentiles shall come to thy light, and kings to the brightness of thy rising...

Many will flock to you. Those that have been rejecting Christ will be drawn to Him in you! Look for it.

Look at Some of These Promises...

*But ye are a chosen generation, a royal priesthood, an holy nation, a peculiar people; that ye should shew forth the praises of him who hath called you out of darkness into his marvellous **light** (1 Peter 2:9)*

*The people which sat in darkness saw **great light**; and to them which sat in the region and shadow of death **light** is sprung up. (Matthew 4:16)*

Many who are now in darkness will be drawn to your **light.**

*You are the **light** of the world. A city that is set on an hill cannot be hid. (Matthew 5:14)*

You are the **light!** This is not a metaphor but a powerful truth!

*And the **light** shines in darkness; and the darkness comprehended it not. (John 1:5)*

Many times those who are in darkness will not understand what they are seeing in you or on you. You will have to explain it to them.

*But if we walk in the **light**, as he is in the **light**, we have fellowship one with another, and the blood of Jesus Christ his Son cleans us from all sin. (1 John 1:7)*

We are able to walk in the **light** as He does. Let us do that.

There is nothing like the Word of God. Whether the Rhema Word given through the inspiration of the Holy Spirit or the written Word in our Bibles. Go through these verses and the ones that you chose earlier and meditate on these scriptures. Let them come to life within you. Let them be life within you. Allow Holy Spirit to give you revelation and wisdom concerning light.

A Prayer

Father,

I thank you for this revelation you have given me. I receive this revelation of your light. I receive it with all of my being. Let your light fill me to overflowing. Let your light fill me to the depths of my soul. Let my spirit, soul and body be transfigured and transformed by your light and the light of your glory be seen upon me. Father may this light that I carry, this light that I am transform the world around me and cause many to come to Christ. May I be clothed with your light and let there be no darkness within me. Father make your presence known in a mighty way to those around me. Let this revelation unfold more every day and may I grow in wisdom and the knowledge of your will .

In Jesus' name

Engaging the Kingdom – Divesting the Garment of Flesh

When you rise in the morning, after you have consecrated yourself and your day to the Lord, do this step of faith. Stand up and close your eyes. Acknowledge the truth that you are a being of light and take a step forward. As you step forward, picture yourself in your imagination as stepping out of your natural body, leaving it behind you and seeing yourself as a being of light. Then spend some time examining your body of light. See how it radiates and lights up the area around you. Feel what this body of light feels like. As you engage all of your spiritual senses to learn about your true being, really see and feel the experience as powerfully as you can.

When you engage your imagination in this way, it may be difficult at first to sustain this for an extended amount of time. You could start with five minutes and increase the amount of time. By spending more time in the revelation and awareness of who you are, it will bring an overwhelming awareness of the reality of it.

The sanctified imagination is a bridge from the natural realm to the spiritual realm. At first, this bridge may seem quite long. But as you engage your imagination with greater frequency and time spent it literally becomes a door.

As you do this exercise, or step of faith, record the time invested and the results as best you can. Do this for **at least thirty days** and you will be greatly blessed by what God does. Then when you realize how powerful this is, you will do it naturally every day .

I pray that you continue to do this and record what God does in your journal or notebook.

Engaging the Kingdom - Seeing the Light

This little exercise lets you engage your spiritual senses in a slightly different way to see that you are a being of light. In a quiet and dark atmosphere, such as dusk or dawn, hold out your hand in front of you. (You could do this before bed or before rising or while in your prayer chair) Imagine your light exuding from your arm or hand. Now as you imagine this, look just to the left or right of your hand. Do not look directly at it, but allow yourself to see it in your peripheral vision. As you do this, there will come a point, usually quite quickly that you will see a slight glow around your hand. Acknowledge this glow and look at it in your peripheral vision. Move your hand around a bit and watch the light shift around your hand. Many times as you do this it will create light trails that come from your hand. Again, this is something that increases as you engage it more. The light will become more obvious and intense and your awareness will only continue to increase.

Engaging the Kingdom – Stretch forth Your Hand

This is similar to the first example, but it's something that you can do anywhere at virtually any time. Stretch out your hand and envision your hand as light. Again, utilize your sanctified imagination to watch the light. Watch it move and pulse. Watch it's colors and hues, watch the glow increase as you focus your intention upon it. (Remember that faith will bring increase and manifestation.) Feel the power and electricity flowing through your hand. Be aware as you do this, that this is light that you can release to affect the world around you. And indeed that is something we are supposed to do. Do these things also a few minutes every day and they will bring great fruit.

Always remember, we do these things as steps of faith while **submitting to Holy Spirit who leads and guides us. We are in training. The Lord is teaching us to walk in the reality of who we really are for the Kingdom of God. This is our time to shine as we do **His will**, for **His purpose** and for **His Kingdom.**

Then answered Jesus and said unto them, Verily, verily, I say unto you, The Son can do nothing of himself, but what he seeth the Father do: for what things soever he doeth, these also doeth the Son likewise. (John 5:19)

Let's be like Jesus.

For more resources and information go to

www.stillwatersinternatinalministries.org

Also Available...

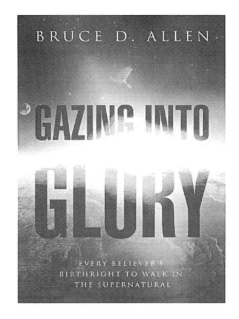

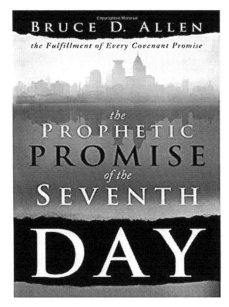
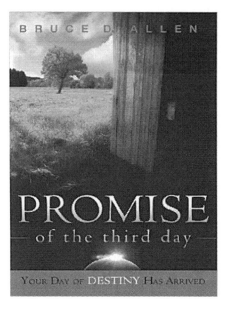

Made in the USA
Middletown, DE
05 January 2018